STUDY THROUGH THE BOOK OF JOHN

A VERSE-BY-VERSE LOOK AT THE GOSPEL OF JOHN

REBECCA BARRON

WESTBOW
PRESS®
A DIVISION OF THOMAS NELSON
& ZONDERVAN

WestBow Press books may be ordered through booksellers or by contacting:

WestBow Press
A Division of Thomas Nelson & Zondervan
1663 Liberty Drive
Bloomington, IN 47403
www.westbowpress.com
844-714-3454

ISBN: 979-8-3850-0078-4 (sc)
ISBN: 979-8-3850-0079-1 (e)

Library of Congress Control Number: 2023911647

Print information available on the last page.

WestBow Press rev. date: 09/14/2023

INTRODUCTION: THE BOOK OF JOHN

There are four gospels, written by Matthew, Mark, Luke, and John. Of the four, it is generally accepted that the book of John was written last. Some unique things stand out about this book. For example, there is no genealogy included for Jesus, no mention of Jesus's teaching in parables, and not a word about the transfiguration (especially interesting when you consider that John was among the few actually there).

Equally of note are things included in John's account and not in the others. John writes about Jesus's first miracle and dedicates a whole chapter to the healing of the man born blind, including the reaction of the Pharisees. We would not know about the resurrection of Lazarus if it were not for the book of John.

The book is divided into twenty-one chapters and scholars date its writing somewhere between AD 85 and 95. Whereas the first three gospels center around Jesus's ministry in Galilee, John focuses much more on what Jesus said and did in Jerusalem. He presents Jesus as the Son of God in His own words and records long discourses of Jesus about Himself.

Beginning in Chapter 12, the final ten chapters of the Book of John deal with the last week of Jesus's earthly life, the crucifixion, and post-resurrection. Almost half the book is devoted to this period.

In reading John, we have a firsthand account from someone who actually heard Jesus's voice audibly on a daily basis for three years. We can hear Jesus's inflection, His pauses,

His laugh, and His expressions. We are presented with a remarkable opportunity to experience what John felt most important for us to know about his friend, his Savior, his Jesus.

THE APOSTLE JOHN

Longstanding tradition holds that John the apostle was the writer of the book of John. Because of this, we're going to start our study by looking at what the Bible says about John and the facts we can use to put together a profile of this close friend of Jesus. This is not meant to be an all-inclusive study of John, but just enough to give us a foundation to build upon.

JOHN'S FAMILY LIFE

1. Matthew 4:21 tells us the names of John's father and brother. Write their names here.

2. In looking first at Matthew 27:56 and then Mark 15:40, we seem to have been given John's mother's name. What is it?

It has been speculated because of John 19:25 that she was Mary's (the mother of Jesus) sister, making John a first cousin to Jesus, but it is only conjecture.

JOHN'S PROFESSIONAL LIFE

3. From the verse in question 1, what is John's vocation at the time he is called to follow Jesus?

4. What are the brothers doing when Jesus sees them on the boat?

> One of the most important skills of fishermen was making and mending nets. Made of linen, a common fabric used in the ancient Near East, these nets had to be carefully cleaned and dried each day or they would quickly rot and wear out. The majority of a fisherman's life probably was spent mending nets (Luke 5:2). Net weights, small pieces of stone with holes drilled in them, were fastened to the bottom of the nets. This too took time. Fishermen also had to be skilled, of course, in the use of the nets in fishing for various types of fish [1]

5. Read Matthew 4:18–22 and Mark 1:16–20. List some facts about John, other than those we've mentioned above, that appear in these passages.

---

[1] "They Left Their Nets Behind," That the World May Know, accessed April 18, 2023, https://www.thattheworldmayknow.com/they-left-their-nets-behind.

6. From Luke 5:10, we get a little bit more information about the relationship between John and Peter. What are your thoughts about Jesus calling them into the ministry at the same time?

7. What qualities do you think a fisherman would possess that would also be beneficial in his new vocation as a disciple of Jesus?

8. John's path in life was already set when it was interrupted by a call from Jesus. List another example in the Bible (New Testament or Old) where a personal encounter with the Lord altered a person's life in a similar way.

One thing I know: that though I was blind, now I see.
—JOHN 9:25B

JOHN'S TIME WITH JESUS

9. John's name is always mentioned in the first four in lists of the twelve disciples (Matt. 10:2, Mark 3:17, Luke 6:14, Acts 1:13). He is even part of a group of three disciples set apart by the Lord on occasion, indicating a close relationship. Write at least two (more if you have time) references and describe the scene in Matthew, Mark, Luke, and/or John when this "inner three" are particularly involved with Jesus.

10. Choose one of your examples from the previous question, read the account again, and think about John specifically. Based on the facts you know of John, write anything you observe or might be able to conclude about him from the example you chose (i.e., what he saw, what he did, his reaction to what Jesus did).

11. Jesus gave James and John nicknames. Write what they are from Mark 3:17.

12. What conclusions can we draw about these brothers with a description like that?

13. Take a look at the following references and write who is involved, what the motive might have been behind the question or statement, and Jesus's response to what was being asked or said.

Mark 9:38–41:

Mark 10:35–41:

Luke 9:51–56:

14. The Lord knows us. He knows our personalities, our weaknesses, our strengths, where we're vulnerable, and where we're confident. He will use all of these things to His glory, if we allow Him the freedom to do so in our lives. Think about this for you personally. What does this mean in your own life?

15. It is generally accepted that "the disciple whom Jesus loved" (John 13:23, 19:26, 20:2, and 21:7, 20, 24) was John himself. He does not describe himself in those exact terms until the Last Supper in Chapter 13. The longer we walk with Jesus, the more we come to realize His heart for us. Using Scripture to back up your answer, write about how we know Jesus desires that each of us would describe ourselves as "the one whom He loves?"

JOHN'S WRITTEN CONTRIBUTION TO THE BIBLE

Five books in the Bible are attributed to John as the human author: the Gospel of John, 1, 2, and 3 John, and Revelation. In each case, the traditional view that the apostle was the author of these books can be traced to writers in the second century. Neither the Gospel nor the epistles identify their authors by name. Modern scholarship has raised questions about the credibility of this tradition, and discussion of these matters continues. Many would agree, however, that the strongest case can be made for the apostolic authorship of Revelation, followed in order by the Gospel and epistles (1, 2, and 3 John).[2]

Church tradition holds that John remained in Jerusalem after the death of Christ and took Jesus's mother into his home there. After the destruction of Jerusalem, he moved to Ephesus. By this time, Ephesus had become the center of the growing Christian population. While there, he was banished to the Isle of Patmos (Rev. 1:9). He was allowed to return to Ephesus, where he penned the five books we accredit to him in our Bible.[3]

---

[2] Trent C. Butler, *Holman Bible Dictionary* (Nashville, TN: Holman Bible Publishers, 1991), 804.

[3] Henry H. Halley, *Halley's Bible Handbook* (Grand Rapids, MI: Zondervan, 1996), 671, 683.

16. Love is a dominant theme in the Gospel of John and that thread runs through 1 John as well. This seems to be one of the things he remembered most about his time with Jesus. He wanted those who would read his writings to remember it too. Why is this significant to note before beginning a study on one of John's books?

17. As mentioned earlier, one of John's distinctive characteristics is that he includes more dialogue from Jesus than in the other three Gospels. John used Jesus's own words to tell His story. How can knowing this help us as we study the Word?

18. Earlier in the study, we discussed briefly the relationship between John and Peter. All the gospels record Peter's denial of Jesus, but John's is the only gospel to detail Jesus's restoration of Peter after His resurrection. Read this account in John 21:1–17. (In this account, note that the Sea of Tiberius is another name for the Sea of Galilee.) In your opinion, what are some reasons John included this?

19. John gives his purpose for writing this book in John 20:31. What reason(s) does he give?

Beloved, let us love one another.
—1 JOHN 4:7

JOHN CHAPTER 1

Each of the four gospels begins a different way. Matthew starts with a genealogy of Jesus beginning with Abraham. Mark introduces us to John the Baptist. Luke begins his book with John the Baptist's parents and details how they were told of his upcoming birth. However, John opens his gospel with the words, "In the beginning." These are the first words of the entire Bible itself. Nothing happened prior to what John was getting ready to pen.

READ JOHN 1:1–5

In verse 1, "the Word" is used three times. This is translated from the word *logos* in Greek. Philosophers of the day said this was "the thought," but John knew it was more than "a thought;" there had to be a thinker. John does not build up to the most important thing; he *begins* with a primary truth. *Logos* literally means "the spoken word." Jesus is "the spoken word" and that "spoken word" was in the beginning. Before there was anything, He was. John gives us an answer to the basic question, "Who is Jesus?"

When we study the book of John, we are not just studying the teachings of Jesus. John wants to make it abundantly clear right from the beginning of his book that our foundation is in knowing *who* He is.

We use words to communicate. We use words to express something to someone else. In order to pass a thought or feeling on to another, we must use words. When this idea is placed next to verse 1, there is nothing in the universe with more depth.

1. What three things does verse 1 tell us about "the Word"?

JOHN CHAPTER 1

2. Go to Genesis 1:1. The word for *God* in this verse is the Hebrew word *Elohiym*, which is the plural form. We might miss that in English, but there is no mistaking what John 1:2 states. Where was Jesus at creation?

3. Why is this truth so important?

4. Verse 3 tells us that not only was Jesus present at creation, He was an active participant in it. Take a look at verse 3 again and then turn to Colossians 1:16. How does the verse in Colossians expand on this thought?

5. John 1:4–5 introduces us to the idea of Jesus as the light. Later, in John 8:12 and 9:5, he records Jesus saying of Himself, "I am the light of the world." What are some things that Jesus declares about Himself by calling Himself "the light"?

READ JOHN 1:6–13

6. In this passage, John switches gears for a moment. Who is being referred to in verse 6?

7. What was this man's purpose (verses 7–8)?

We have terrific detail of the beginning of John the Baptist's life recorded for us in the book of Luke. Read Luke 1:5–17.

8. Write Luke 1:16 here.

To make ready a people prepared for the Lord.
—LUKE 1:17

There are not very many people in the Bible that we have the privilege of knowing from the womb to the grave. John the Baptist would be one. We don't have a lot of detail on many years of his life, but we do have snippets recorded about how he came to this earth and how he left it (Matt. 14; Mark 6; Luke 9).

9. From before he was conceived, John the Baptist's reason for living was laid out for his parents. His entire life was literally wrapped up in telling people about Jesus and "to bear witness of that Light." Why do you think John actually tells us in verse 8 when he writes *"he* was not that Light" (emphasis mine)?

10. John was writing to a Jewish and Gentile audience. Look at Isaiah 49:6b. The phrase "every man" in John 1:9 is crucial for us. It relates to why and to whom He came for. Can you think of other verses that tell us that Jesus came for both Jews and Gentiles?

11. Verse 10 is amazing because it spells out for us that the one who *made* the world inserted Himself *into* the world, but the world _____ _____ _____ _____.

12. Verse 11 takes the thought a step further. Jesus came to His own and His own _____ _____ _____ _____.

13. In both cases (verses 10 and 11), Jesus was rejected as the Messiah. He was not recognized for who He was by the very world He had created and the people He had chosen. What are some reasons that people, even in our own time, do not acknowledge who Jesus is?

14. The key word in verse 12 is "but" because it signals a change is coming. What does the verse say is the promise for those who do receive Him?

15. A popular thought in our time is that "we are all God's children." Verses 12 and 13 are one passage in the Bible that clearly refutes that statement. Can you think of other verses that would reiterate the truth of John 1:12–13?

READ JOHN 1:14–18

"And the Word became flesh and dwelt among us." This is the incarnation. I heard it explained this way in a message years ago: "God tabernacled with us…He 'tent camped.'" What an incredibly beautiful picture of the sacrifice of Jesus. Obviously, this thought only scratches the surface of what our Lord gave up to put on flesh and live on Earth. Nevertheless, it at least puts us in a place where we can begin to contemplate what He was choosing to give up for a time.

16. Write out the following verses.

Philippians 2:6:

Philippians 2:7:

Philippians 2:8:

17. Whether you like to camp or not, you would have to agree that there are certain things that you choose to give up when you decide to take on this activity. By placing Himself within the confines of flesh, list some things Jesus (the Word) chose according to the verses listed above.

18. "And we beheld His glory." John saw His glory. The disciples saw His glory. Many, many others saw His glory, but the word "beheld" implies so much more than simply seeing. The word in the Greek means to "look upon, view attentively, contemplate."[4] *Jesus allowed Himself to be contemplated by His own creation.* Write some words or phrases that come to your mind after reading this thought.

19. In verse 15, John the apostle cites an example of the words of John the Baptist that point back to Jesus and away from himself: "He who comes after me is preferred before me, for He was before me." List two other examples of this habit of John the Baptist we find in the gospels.

20. List at least one thing that each of the following verses says specifically about Jesus:

John 1:16:

John 1:17:

John 1:18:

The fact that we have access to all the things you have written above about Jesus and through Jesus should make us thankful—very thankful.

Behold what manner of love the Father has bestowed on
us, that we should be called children of God!
—1 JOHN 3:1A

---

4 "John 1 (KJV) - And the Word was made." Blue Letter Bible. Accessed 25 May, 2023. https://www.blueletterbible.org/kjv/jhn/1/14/s_998014

READ JOHN 1:19–28

There was a lot of talk about John the Baptist. He was unconventional in his lifestyle (Matt. 3:4 and Mark 1:6) and he preached a radical message of repentance (Matt. 3:2 and Mark 1:4). It is not surprising that the Jews sent their religious leaders to find out more about him. If you picture the scene, it is fascinating. A staunch group of men gathers to question a guy who does not fit their mold, but seems to know something—something that was hitting a nerve with the people. Who was he?

21. First, John the Baptist clearly states three times who he is *not*. In answer to their questions in verses 19 and 21, who does he say he isn't?

"The Prophet" refers to God's promise through Moses in Deuteronomy 18:15 that a prophet would come. "Based on this passage, they expected another prophet to come, and wondered if John was not he."[5] --David Guzik, Blue Letter Bible Commentary

However, in verse 23, John quotes Isaiah 40:3 as his answer to their questions. Amazing! To know with confidence that the words of the prophet Isaiah were written about you is incredible! He is the "herald" for the King…the King of Kings and Lord of Lords. Everything John the Baptist did or said pointed back to Jesus.

22. Because we have the whole account, it is a bit difficult to put ourselves in their shoes while they are trying to figure out John the Baptist. The priests and Levites questioned him. Verse 24 reveals that the Pharisees had their own questions for him about baptism. The Jewish religious leaders of the day baptized Gentiles who wanted to adopt the Jewish faith, but John the Baptist was baptizing Jews. This is another example of the radical things John was doing. What do you think the motivation for all their questioning was?

---

[5] Guzik, D. "Study Guide for Deuteronomy 18 by David Guzik." Blue Letter Bible. Last Modified 6/2022. https://www.blueletterbible.org/comm/guzik_david/study-guide/deuteronomy/deuteronomy-18.cfm

23. In John's reply in verses 26 and 27, he not only points *to* Jesus, he also points *away* from himself. List some things that John wanted them to note about himself from these verses.

READ JOHN 1:29–34

If they didn't have enough to think about that day, the very next day, John the Baptist gave all the crowds a bit more to ponder.

24. What title does John the Baptist give to Jesus in verse 29?

25. What was His purpose, as noted in verse 29?

The Jews were very familiar with the concept of the lamb and the sacrifice. The blood of their sacrifices could only *cover* sin. This Lamb was going to "take *away* the sin." Jesus came to take away the sin of the world. That is a fact. He did it. However, I only receive the benefit from that fact if I have accepted what He did as a personal payment for my personal sin. With this public declaration, John the Baptist cast a shadow of things to come that would stretch into eternity.

However, these things would come later. John the Baptist would not have known how many days, months, or years it would be. He only declared things that had been revealed to him. He was a living, breathing witness of who He was/is.

26. In verses 32 through 34, John the Baptist refers to Jesus's baptism, but John (the apostle) does not record His baptism. Read Matthew 3:13–17 and Mark 1:9–11 right now for the details of that event. John the Baptist appears to give us some insight into what was going on from his point of view during the baptism of Jesus. List everything from verses 32 through 34 that John is "bearing witness" to about Jesus.

READ JOHN 1:35–42

John the apostle recorded events that happened within a few days of each other (verses 29 and 35) as he observed John the Baptist and what was happening around him.

Verse 35 raises the question, who are these two disciples of John the Baptist? One is definitely Andrew, Peter's brother (verse 40), but the other is unnamed. Almost every scholar believes this man to be John, the author of the book. A few speculate it may be Philip. Their reasons can be summed up in this way. First, John the apostle has a habit of never mentioning himself by name in his book. Second, he painstakingly includes names throughout his narrative; to leave someone unnamed besides himself appears to be out of character. That said, he is unnamed, so all is just speculation.

27. What is the definition of *disciple*?

28. Why do you think John the Baptist had disciples at this time?

29. In verse 36, John the Baptist does what he has always done: point people to Jesus using the phrase "Lamb of God." In fact, the wording implies that it was on John the Baptist's word that these two left him and followed Jesus. In a practical sense, the best leaders point people to Jesus. How does Jesus respond in verse 38?

30. As of this moment, these two had a new leader. They were now on a different path. Jesus knows all things so, in your opinion, why did He begin with the question, "What do you seek?"

31. Personal: If Jesus were to audibly ask that same question of you today, what would you say?

32. What a beautiful invitation by our Lord in verse 39 with the words, "Come and see." What are some things that this phrase tells us about the heart of Jesus?

33. The verse goes on to tell us that they "came," they "saw," and they "remained" based on that appeal by Jesus. After spending even this short amount of time with Jesus, what does Andrew do (verses 41 and 42)?

34. We know that John and Peter had a relationship prior to their time with Jesus (Luke 5:10), so the fact that John records what Jesus had to say about Peter's name in verse 42 is just so real. He's the only disciple who will have a name change. What are some reasons Jesus may have done this when He first met him?

READ JOHN 1:43–51

35. In verse 43, the phrase "wanted to go" (NKJV) gives us a glimpse into the mind of Jesus. In some other versions, the phrase is "decided to go" (NLT) or "purposed to go" (NASB). There was purpose to every single thing that Jesus did or said. We can assume that His purpose in going to Galilee this time was to find Philip. Write John 15:16 here.

We probably all have a fear, on some level, of not being chosen. That fear will creep in during all stages of our lives: being selected out of a lineup for a team game in elementary school or receiving that promotion at work. This fear will actually drive us to do things to stand out. This text gives us no indication of anything that Philip is *doing* that makes him different from anyone else around him. If we can grasp the personal message of the first half of John 15:16 for ourselves, it will change our lives.

36. Jesus says, "Follow Me" to Philip. What does Philip do (verse 45)?

37. Amazing! What do you think motivated Philip to tell Nathanael so soon after being called?

38. Nathanael gives Philip a bit (a very small bit) of opposition, as recorded in verse 46. Moving past our own prejudgments is sometimes a roadblock for us in seeing Jesus. What is Philip's answer?

39. Those words are really the answer to any question we have or any emotion we feel: "Come and see." At this point, we know that Philip hadn't really *seen* much at all as far as Jesus was concerned. What do you think made him make such a bold statement to Nathanael?

40. Verses 47 through 51 record this short conversation between Jesus and Nathanael. It is a remarkable discourse between the two. Read these verses out loud and write a few observations about the passage that stand out to you.

So ends chapter 1 of the book of John. This book is the result of John's time with Jesus. May our time spent in this book be blessed.

Thanks be to God for His indescribable gift.
—2 Corinthians 9:15

JOHN CHAPTER 2

The humanity of Jesus is sometimes overlooked as we read the pages of the gospels. We cannot, however, study the book of John without continually coming back to this truth because it so clearly contrasts with the focus of John's book, which is Jesus—the Son of God. God in flesh. The "Word *became* flesh."

Chapter 2 opens with a social event: a wedding. In general, the Lord has made us social people. I don't mean just Americans; I mean as people we tend to gather in groups. We congregate for various reasons, sometimes for good and productive reasons and sometimes for not so good or particularly productive reasons.

Nevertheless, we do like our celebrations, don't we?

****

READ JOHN 2:1–12

There is a lot of room for speculation in this account and we'll do a bit of that. We will also pull out some solid, practical applications from these verses and the passage as a whole.

Let's take a look at the account from five points of view: Mary, the disciples, Jesus, the servants, and the master.

MARY

1. We can be certain that Mary wanted Jesus to do something about the dilemma, although the text is not specific about what she wanted Him to do. Why do you think she approached Him?

2. What is the purpose of a miracle?

3. It is probably fair to say that Mary's relationship to Jesus gave her unique access to Him on this occasion. If she was hoping for a miracle, on what was she basing that expectation?

4. It was with that hope she addressed the servants. What did she tell them (verse 5)?

5. It does not appear in verse 4 that He would be doing anything at all about the problem she presented to Him. Yet, her words in verse 5 reveal something else. How would you describe the attitude behind her response?

THE DISCIPLES

6. From Chapter 1, we know the group of disciples who had been called so far. Refer back to Chapter 1 and list their names.

7. They had no way of knowing what the significance of this wedding would be. In the years that were to come, the disciples would sometimes play a direct role in carrying out the miracles of Jesus, but not this time. They were just observing on this day. Again, referring back to chapter 1, what were the only things they really knew for sure about Jesus at that point?

8. They had a *foundation* of belief, but now Jesus was beginning to build their faith, trust, and hope that He was who they believed Him to be. What do you think the phrase "His disciples believed in Him" means in verse 11?

9. As the group begins to travel in verse 12, what are some words that might describe the mindset of those heading to Capernaum?

10. Why do you think He might have chosen Cana rather than a big religious hub like Jerusalem for this first miracle? Cana was a small town between Capernaum and Nazareth in Galilee. It was the hometown of Nathanael (John 21:2) and where the nobleman sought out Jesus to heal his son (John 4:46).

11. Why a wedding as opposed to a religious feast?

12. What are your thoughts about the timing of this miracle? He had just begun His public ministry with His baptism.

13. Because we are not given answers to these specific questions, we can only speculate on the Lord's reasons for the time and place of these events. There are things we do know about Jesus through the Scripture that can set a backdrop for the thoughts we have about the account. What are some verses to back up what you know about Jesus to support your responses for questions 10 through 12 above? Write the references here.

14. In the text, we have Jesus answering His mother and then addressing the servants. We cannot impose our own social mores upon the text, especially in looking at His response to his mother in verse 4. We can be completely confident that Jesus's response to *any* situation was exactly as He intended it to be. He almost immediately set into motion the solution to the problem presented to Him in verse 3. What are some observations you can make about His instructions in verses 7 and 8?

THE SERVANTS

15. This group had an integral part in this miracle. It is probably worth noting that they were physically closer than anyone else to the actual miracle, yet we don't know a single name for any of them. What were their two commands from Jesus?

1)

2)

16. Write out a job description for a servant.

17. Obedience is the number one characteristic of a good servant, and obedience to Jesus allows the servants to observe things that others at the wedding missed. This truth is hidden in verse 9. Why do you think they were allowed to see this miracle from start to finish?

THE MASTER

The word "master" in verse 8 is the Greek word *architriklinos* which means "the superintendent of the dining room, a table master."[6] We don't know exactly who he was, but we do know that he was in some kind of authority at the wedding. His importance to the account is only because of his announcement to the bridegroom in verse 10.

18. In your own words, what does he declare to the bridegroom?

19. He doesn't have any personal contact with Jesus that is recorded. He tasted the wine brought to him by the servants (at Jesus's command) and then made his assumption. The master doesn't credit Jesus with what has happened. Why do you think John records his statement about the wine?

20. Write a practical application that we can take from each of the perspectives.

Mary:

The Disciples:

Jesus:

---

[6] "G755 - architriklinos - Strong's Greek Lexicon (nkjv)." Blue Letter Bible. Accessed 25 May, 2023. https://www.blueletterbible.org/lexicon/g755/nkjv/tr/0-1/

The Servants:

The Master:

READ JOHN 2:13–22

21. Verse 13 gives us a backdrop for what is happening in Jerusalem by telling us that it was the "Passover of the Jews." This would mean that there were thousands of people visiting the city and a particularly crowed temple mount. Passover was part of their heritage. It was a celebration of remembrance. In Deuteronomy 16:1–6, the Lord reminds them (and us) of the when, why, and where related to the Passover. Read the passage in Deuteronomy and then write out the following regarding Passover.

When:

Why:

Where:

It appears to be in part of the "how" (verse 14) that Jesus encounters a scene that demands His swift and immediate attention. Probably many things were disturbing to Him about this picture. The noise and chaos of the haggling certainly could have been part of the problem. The fact that this was taking place in the "Court of the Gentiles," the only place non-Jews could come and worship, was not lost on Jesus either.

However, the real problem is spelled out in an excerpt from the *Expositor's Greek Testament*.

> It was of course a great convenience to the worshippers to be able to procure on the spot all requisites for sacrifice. Some of them might not know what sacrifice was required for their particular offence, and though the priest at their own home might inform them, still the officiating examiner in the Temple might reject the animal they brought as unfit; and probably

would, if it was his interest to have the worshippers buying on the spot...
But especially was it offensive to make the Temple service a hardship and
an offence to the people of God. [7]

Jesus cares a great deal about His people and He takes offense at leadership that would misrepresent His heart before them.

22. From verses 15 and 16, write out some things that we learn about Jesus.

23. His disciples were looking at Jesus and were reminded of Psalm 69:9 (verse 17), so the scene made an impression. How do you think His disciples were feeling upon seeing His reaction inside the temple walls?

The crowds were taking notice too. There were so many people, an explosion of emotion, a whip being brandished, and tables being slung out of the way. The question of verse 18 was one of authority and certainly was reasonable to them considering what they had just witnessed. Had Jesus wanted to draw a crowd, He chose the perfect place and time to do just that. However, this was just the beginning. There would be many more questions from the crowds and many more replies from Jesus.

24. What does Jesus refer to by His answer to the crowd in verse 19 (verse 21)?

---

[7] "Expositor's Greek Testament." John 2:14. Bible Hub. Accessed May 25, 2023. https://biblehub.com/commentaries/egt/john/2.htm

It is worth noting that John wrote his account many years after these events actually happened, but He remembered this scene very well. Clearly, the crowd did not understand what Jesus was referring to in His reply. They must have been thinking (as we would be) while they looked around, "The temple? Herod's temple? It would surely *not* be destroyed, but even if it was, could it be raised up in three days? Impossible. Just look at it!"

25. Three years later, after His triumphal entry, Jesus cleared the temple again, much in the same manner (Matt. 21:12–13; Mark 11:15–17; Luke 19:45–18). Think for a minute about what was *supposed* to be happening within the temple walls. List some of those things here along with at least one verse or passage that speaks of each.

26. The moneychangers were distracting people from the things listed above. What are some things that could distract us from worship in our own sanctuaries on Sunday mornings?

READ JOHN 2:23–25

27. Verse 23 says that "many believed," but what was the reason for their belief?

28. Our flesh wants to base our beliefs on what we can see. We want explanations that make sense. We like it when things line up in a reasonable way. Why do you think this is so appealing?

29. What is the problem with believing based solely on what we see?

30. Conversely, what does the Bible say about how we are to live?

Examine me, O Lord, and prove me; try my mind and my heart.
—Psalm 26:2

JOHN CHAPTER 3

This chapter contains one of the most memorized verses in the entire Bible. We teach it to our preschoolers and recite it continually in our children's ministry classes. It is interesting that a verse that explains the Gospel simply (John 3:16) is found within a conversation between Jesus and a well-educated man of arguably the most religious sect of the day. Such a beautiful truth is brought so low a child can grasp it, yet it is so deep that it is hard to comprehend the fullness it contains.

Throughout the book of John, we witness many discourses between Jesus and the people He came to save. They represent a variety of ages from different nations and backgrounds, but He remains constant—always the same. It does not seem unusual when He addresses groups of thousands or teaches His close circle of twelve a wonderful truth. When He has chosen to take a precious moment to be one-on-one with a person, we should take special care to note this because His heart for the "one" means He has a heart for you and me individually, too.

READ JOHN 3:1–21

1. List everything we know (or could ascertain) about Nicodemus from verses 1 and 2.

2. Why do you think he came to see Jesus "by night"?

3. In looking at verse 2, what do you think Nicodemus's purpose was in coming to see Jesus? What was he hoping for?

4. John 3:3 is the first time we see the phrase "born again." For the Jews, their lineage was very important. Being descendants of Abraham, in their minds, was enough to assure them that they were good with God. Within just a few minutes, Jesus was beginning to break apart what Nicodemus thought he knew and could count on. Has Jesus ever shown you something that needed to change in your own thinking? If so, share a little about it here.

5. Nicodemus is confused, but praise God he questions Jesus further because now we share in the benefit of His answers. Write out verse 6 here.

6. In stating that these are two separate occurrences, Jesus makes it clear that we are not "all God's children," as is popular in our day. List at least two other verses or passages in the New Testament that would echo this very important truth.

7. In verses 7 and 8, Jesus seems to be reminding Nicodemus that there are things that he believes and doesn't question all around him. Jesus knew exactly how to communicate with him. Nicodemus was an educated man and he liked to think things through, but his very life depended on the questions he was asking Jesus at that moment. Nicodemus asked basically two questions. What are they?

1)

2)

8. One thing that this narrative definitely shows us is that Jesus is not put off by our questions. Make no mistake, however: He is very aware of the states of our hearts in asking. What do you think He sees in Nicodemus that pleases Him?

9. The words in verse 9 are the last recorded by Nicodemus. He remained quiet as Jesus explained exactly what he needed to know next. He challenged Nicodemus in verse 12 with the words, "you do not believe." Nicodemus was *supposed* to believe. He was *supposed* to know these things already (verse 10). What do you think has kept him from belief up to this point?

10. Sometimes our preconceived notions about certain verses or passages will block our understanding of what the Lord has for us. Has there been a time when this was true in your own life?

11. What does Jesus state about His authority in verse 13?

12. Turn to Numbers 21 and read through the account in 21:4–9. In your own words, state what happened.

13. Because we live on this side of the cross, the comparison that Jesus makes is easier for us to grasp. How does belief play a part in the account in the book of Numbers?

14. How does belief factor into being born again (verse 15)?

15. Read John 3:16 out loud. Now, read it again. Now, read it once more. Choose a phrase in this verse that sticks out to you, maybe one you never noticed before. Write the phrase here and then explain why you chose it.

16. We can see John 3:16 on signs at nationally televised football games and on the walls of our church nurseries. Why do you think this is such a popular verse?

17. What condemns us (verses 17–18)?

18. What are some examples of things people believe in for salvation instead of Jesus?

19. Jesus talks of light and darkness in verses 19 through21. In the most practical sense, what is the purpose of light? (Don't over think it; just write some things that come to mind.)

20. We already touched briefly in chapter 1 about Jesus being "the Light." It is really so much better to be in the light than it is to be in the dark. Yet, verse 19 says, "men loved darkness rather than light." From verses 19 and 20, what are the reasons for this?

21. If something (anything) is "exposed," what are some options of what can happen next?

22. In verse 21, the word "but" is an important one because it gives the alternative to verse 20. Remember who Jesus is speaking to at that moment: a Pharisee, a "teacher of Israel." Why do you think Jesus included the phrase "done in God" in a conversation with one of the most religious men of their day?

23. What is one practical truth you personally can take away from listening in on this conversation between Jesus and Nicodemus?

READ JOHN 3:22–36

We have the paths of Jesus and John the Baptist crossing again in this passage. Both were baptizing (although not Jesus personally; see John 4:2) and it appears that both had followers.

24. In your opinion, should John the Baptist still have had disciples (verse 25)? Why or why not?

The word translated "disciple" in this verse and verse 22 is the Greek word *mathetes*, which means "a learner." *Vine's Expository Dictionary* expounds on this thought, stating that "a 'disciple' was not only a pupil, but an adherent; hence they are spoken of as imitators of their teacher."[8]

25. In light of his declaration about Jesus (John 1:29-34), do you think his preaching would have been different at this time? Why or why not?

26. In verse 26, John's disciples inform him of something that they thought was a real problem, namely, "John, you're losing people. They're going over to Jesus." John the Baptist's reply in verse 27 is perfectly practical. How can the truth of verse 27 prevent jealousy or pride from taking over our thought processes?

27. So many times the enemy, our culture, or even our friends want to frighten us into thinking that we're losing what we have or we don't have enough. Certainly, John the Baptist had reason to think highly of himself, but he shows us over and over that he is confident in his calling and his purpose. In your own words, write how John the Baptist's joy is being fulfilled (verse 29).

---

[8] Vine, W. "Disciple - Vine's Expository Dictionary of New Testament Words." Blue Letter Bible. Last Modified 24 Jun, 1996. https://www.blueletterbible.org/search/Dictionary/viewTopic.cfm

28. Verse 30 is for every one of us who knows Jesus—there should be more of Him, less of us. This is simple to say, but sometimes hard to nail down exactly what it looks like. Use this space to write down some practical ways He can increase and you can decrease.

29. Verses 31 through 36 are all about Jesus. List at least one truth from each of these verses that is directly related to Jesus Himself.

Verse 31:

Verse 32:

Verse 33:

Verse 34:

Verse 35:

Verse 36:

30. We all know people who do not believe in who Jesus is. Maybe those people appear to even be prospering by the world's standards. What does the phrase "shall not see life" mean to you?

"I have come that they may have life, and that they may have it more abundantly."
—JOHN 10:10B

JOHN CHAPTER 4

Chapter 4 begins with Jesus traveling north from Judea to Galilee. Along the way, He stops at the city of Sychar, a small town located in Samaria between the two regions. Sychar's "claim to fame," if you will, was its proximity to Jacob's well.

In looking at a map, it makes perfect sense that Jesus would choose to go this way. We would all choose to go this way because it is a straight shot from Judea to Galilee along this road. However, to a Jew—to His disciples—this made absolutely no sense at all. There was a problem, and the Samaritans were the problem.

The Samaritans did have a historical connection to the Jewish people. Generations earlier, the Samaritans were those left behind by the Babylonians when the northern kingdom was conquered. They were not deemed "good enough" to be taken away to the Babylonian empire. As other groups moved into the land, these were the Jews who intermarried with them. Thus, the Samaritans— the "compromised Jews"—were born.

The Samaritans had adopted **some** of the Jewish traditions, but over the years, had rewritten history by saying Mt. Gerizim was where Abraham sacrificed Isaac (rather than Mt. Moriah) making Mt. Gerizim their "Jerusalem." This was their center of worship, but it was a not a place that God had chosen.

This was the mountain that the Samaritan woman in chapter 4 looked at every day. I am blessed to live in an area where I look at mountains every day, but there is no religious significance to my view except that it points to a Creator who loves me enough to place me in a breathtaking area. For the Samaritan woman, the mountain itself connected her to worship.

READ JOHN 4:1–26

1. The Pharisees apparently were keeping track of both Jesus and John the Baptist. In your opinion, why would they care what was going on with either of them?

2. "Therefore, when the Lord knew...He left Judea" (1–3). Because everything the Lord does has a purpose, how do you think these two ideas are related?

3. He "needed" to go (verse 4) is really closer in translation to the phrase "must needs." In fact, in the King James Version, the verse reads exactly that: "He must needs go through Samaria." What are some things this short verse says about the humanity of Jesus?

Geographically, we know where Jesus was going. The text clearly states "a city of Samaria which is called Sychar" (verse 5). Historically, we know something about the area as well, "near the plot of ground that Jacob gave to his son Joseph" (Gen. 48:22). This account is going to center around the *spiritual* significance of the location, both its past and its future.

4. John paints a picture of the scene before beginning his account. What details do we learn from verse 6 alone to help us?

The "sixth hour" was probably around noon. This is the second time so far that John has made note of the exact hour something took place. He also mentions it in verse 1:39.

She came to draw water (verse 7). There is much said in commentaries about why she came in the heat of the day and why she chose this well to draw from. I will not presuppose in this study why she did either. If your own mind goes there, it can add to the dimension of the account. Why we, as women, do what we do is sometimes difficult to nail down. The important part is that she *did* come and the only thing that makes that fact important is who was waiting for her.

5.   What does Jesus show us about Himself by His opening statement to her in verse 7?

6.   He is not only a man, but He is a Jewish man. Jesus is no respecter of persons. He came to this place for her. Make no mistake: the Lord orchestrates practical situations all the time in order to intervene supernaturally. Cite another example of this from any of the four gospels or from your own life.

Thus begins a dialogue between an unnamed woman and God Himself. When she grabbed her water jug and left her house for the well that day, she had no idea that she was going to encounter Jesus. She may have been thinking about "spiritual things." Maybe she glanced up at the mountain, which reminded her she needed to pray and so a quick "prayer" shot across her mind. Maybe, just maybe, she had been too busy before she left to even think about God. Maybe she left later than she had planned to get the water. Maybe it was getting warm out so she needed to get this chore done and out of the way. Maybe she was feeling down because the weight of where she was in her life was too much.

Because I am a woman, none of those scenarios seem odd or unusual to me. I can easily imagine her distracted and preoccupied or determined and focused by the chore at hand, having a list of "to-dos" to complete. The Lord has given us this ability to think about and take care of many things at once.

Here's my point: there is nothing recorded in the text that leads us to believe she did anything special before she arrived at the well. She was simply taking care of a practical task and there was Jesus.

7. She appears to be anxious to engage in conversation. She could have just given Him the drink and been done with it. What do you think was her initial motive in beginning this exchange (verse 9)?

There are differing schools of thought in the commentaries on the last statement in verse 9. Maybe the author is explaining why she asked the question or maybe her own words imply why she asked. Either way, verse 8 shows that there was clearly some interaction between the two groups of people (at least in situations involving business).

8. The NLT translation of verse 10 makes it a bit easier to understand: "Jesus replied, 'If you only knew the gift God has for you and Who you are speaking to, you would ask Me and I would give you living water.'" In essence, Jesus is saying, "If you really knew what was going on here, this exchange would be going quite differently." All of a sudden, this conversation wasn't about a drink. Why do you think He was so quick to make it about the spiritual rather than physical?

9. Based on her reply in verse 11, what do you think piqued her interest most about what Jesus had to say in verse 10? Why?

10. Sometimes, we are more interested in the "gift" than the "giver." However, the giver of "every good gift and every perfect gift" wants us to know that if we recognize who He is, our requests will be for things that satisfy our true needs. Look up each verse below and complete the sentence:

Deuteronomy 12:10: He gives _____

Job 34:29: He gives _____

Psalm 68:35: He gives _____

Psalm 144:10: He gives _____

Psalm 146:7: He gives _____

Proverbs 2:6: He gives _____

Proverbs 3:34: He gives _____

Isaiah 40:29: He gives _____

John 1:9: He gives _____

John 5:21: He gives _____

1 Corinthians 15:57: He gives _____

11. Of the list above, which are you personally in need of the most right now? Take some time to ask Him.

12. You can read verses 11 and 12 in different tones of voice and draw various conclusions about the woman's intention in her comments to Jesus. What are your thoughts about her attitude at this point in the narrative?

13. Jesus knows the thoughts and intents of every heart. Write Psalm 139:2 here.

14. Many times, Jesus will use the practical things around us in order to speak a truth He wants pressed upon our hearts. In this case, He speaks of water (her task at hand). List everything He says about His water in verses 13 and 14.

15. From her response in verse 15, we can see that she is intrigued by what she has heard. What this man is talking about would definitely make her life much easier. Can you imagine never being thirsty again or never having to draw water again? Why do you think we are so desirous of easing our physical difficulties?

16. Verses 16 through 18 seem to be a bit of a side note to the conversation. What reason(s) can you think of that would cause Jesus bring to mention her "husband" at all?

I personally think that Jesus wanted her to say the words "I have no husband" out loud. There is something different about saying the words for our own ears to hear. Our hurt spoken aloud will sometimes stretch our vocabularies to the point that we will search for the perfect sentiment to match what we are trying to communicate. In doing so, we will land on something so deep we didn't even know it was there.

17. The issue was not that she had "no husband." Her relationships with men were out of control. This appears to be her life-dominating sin. What is Jesus's purpose when He calls out our sin?

18. With that, she quickly attempts to take control of the conversation by speaking in "religious" terms. She uses words like "prophet" and "worship" in her reply to Jesus (verses 19–20). What do you think her motivation was in answering this way?

If she was attempting to appear more "righteous" than she really was, I can certainly relate. Sometimes I want people to think I'm more "holy" than I really am, that I'm closer to God than I really am, and that I spend much more time in prayer than I really do. There is a danger in knowing a lot *about* God because it will mask my need to actually *know* God. Maybe when she felt the heaviness of guilt over her life choices, she could sleep at night because she knew this fact: "Our fathers worshiped on this mountain"—the mountain she looked at every day.

She was close—right?
I mean, she was close to God—right?

19. Remember in verse 4 when Jesus "needed to go through Samaria"? Jesus's words in verses 21 through 24 are the reason. He "must needs" tell her these things. From these four verses, make a list of what we learn about "worship" from Jesus Himself.

20. Because worship is something that is God-ordained, we don't get to decide how, when, or where it's done. The Lord dictates every aspect of true worship. Why is it important that we know what is true worship and what is not (either for ourselves or others)?

21. List three or four references (either the Old Testament or the New) that talk about worship (either personal or corporate).

It fascinates me to see that Jesus spoke to this woman about worship. They banter a bit about water. She then brings up worship and the Lord expands on that thought with her. Remember, this is right after He makes it clear to her that He knows her "situation" with the men in her life. She is exposed. She has to know that she couldn't hide anything with this man. No more games. No more putting on a brave face. At this moment, it was just the two of them sitting and talking, a woman and the God of the universe.

Wow.

22. Who does Jesus say that He is in verse 26 (verse 25)?

23. Jesus revealed Himself to her personally. He did not always lay it out so plainly to people face to face. What do you think made her different? What did He see in her in that short conversation the prompted Him to tell her that He was the "Messiah"?

But you are a chosen generation, a royal priesthood, a holy nation,
His own special people, that you may proclaim the praises of Him
who called you out of darkness into His marvelous light.
—1 PETER 2:9

READ JOHN 4:27–38

What a great scene. Jesus is saying, "I who speak to you am He," and then His disciples walk up. They were not allowed into this private conversation. Although they wondered about it, they did not question Him (verse 27).

24. In your opinion, why do you think that John noted this fact for us in verse 27?

25. She "left her waterpot" (verse 28). The thing that brought her there in the first place was forgotten, abandoned, and neglected. It just didn't matter right then. What practical personal application can you make of this for your own life?

26. Why do you think she went to the men (verses 28–29)?

27. An even more interesting question: why do you think they listened and came (verse 30)?

28. "In the meantime," the disciples were preoccupied with the practical need at hand. It's probably fair to say that sometimes we miss the spiritual while being focused on the physical. Jesus takes the opportunity to use it as a teaching moment, however. What does Jesus say is His "food" (verse 34)?

29. What do you think Jesus means by the phrase "to finish His work" (verse 34)?

So when Jesus had received the sour wine, He said, "It is finished!"
—JOHN 19:30

With verses 35 through 38, Jesus gives them a new vision of sorts—a new perspective on sowing and reaping. Both are important and necessary in the fields, but nothing was going to have more lasting ramifications than what He was sending them to do.

30. Who do you think that Jesus refers to in verse 35 by the phrase "others have labored"?

31. Read 1 Corinthians 3:5–9. The practical application for both this passage and the passage in John 4:35–38 is what?

READ JOHN 4:39–42

We don't know the specific needs for every person we will meet. Don't get me wrong. We can know some needs—the needs that they choose to make us aware of. The deep things that the heart cries out for in the darkness are known only by their loving Creator. For this reason, our goal must be to bring people to Jesus.

32. Many believed in Him "because of the word of the woman," but according to verse 41, why did "many more believe"?

33. Each person must have his or her own encounter with Jesus. No one is saved by association. Yet, we know that the Lord chooses to use us sometimes to draw people unto Himself. The Samaritan woman played an important part in this salvation story by telling others who she had met. What does the text tell us she actually said about Him (verses 29 and 39)?

34. It's interesting to me that is what she chose to tell the men. Jesus must have had such a kind demeanor. Her past was not a pretty story and He made it clear to her that it was not going to keep her from knowledge of the Messiah. What else can we surmise about Jesus by expanding on this thought?

READ JOHN 4:43–45

Jesus stayed in Sychar for two days at the urging of the people who lived there (verse 40) and then went north into Galilee (verse 43).

Verse 44 is a curious verse because of the definition of "his own country." Some commentators define Jesus's "own country" as Judea because the place of His birth was Bethlehem, while other commentators explain Jesus's "own country" as Nazareth because it is the place where He was raised and educated. The latter presents a bit of a conundrum as the next verse states that the "Galileans received Him," which appears to contradict verse 44. If "his own country" is Judea, then going north into Galilee as opposed to going south into Judea seems to make sense within the context of verses 44 and 45.

Jews who lived in Galilee would have traveled to Jerusalem for the feasts, but verse 45 goes further and says "the Galileans received Him, having seen all the things He did in Jerusalem at the feast." David Guzik brings up a fascinating point about this verse.

> What did Jesus do that they remembered? His turning of the merchant's tables in the outer courts of the temple (John 2:13–17). Jesus predicted His own miraculous resurrection (John 2:18–22). Also, Jesus performed many other unspecified signs during this time in Jerusalem (John 2:23–25).[9]

At the very least, Jesus must have aroused their curiosity.

---

[9] Guzik, D. "Study Guide for John 4 by David Guzik." Blue Letter Bible. Last Modified 6/2022. https://www.blueletterbible.org/comm/guzik_david/study-guide/john/john-4.cfm

READ JOHN 4:46–54

We end chapter 4 with a beautiful story of healing. A healing takes place, but the account is really about desperation and where it will drive us.

35. Verse 46 says that Jesus went back to Cana, "where He had made the water wine." Many people would have witnessed this miracle since the occasion was a wedding. Are there times when a place is more primed and ready for the supernatural? If so, what makes the difference?

36. Are there things that could be inferred about this particular region because Jesus chose to go back there and ultimately perform another miracle?

37. The word for nobleman is *basilikos* in Greek, which means "of or belong[ing] to a king." He was part of the royal court, connected in some way to the royal household. The word implies high social standing. That didn't matter in relationship to his need. What does verse 47 tell us was the concern that brought him to Jesus?

38. Write as many synonyms for the word *implored* as you can think of.

39. Verse 47 says urgency to me, but not quite desperation—not quite yet. Why do you think Jesus responded the way he did in verse 48?

Now we see desperation. Verse 49 is real. It's raw. It's the cry of a heart with absolutely nowhere else to go. Think about his eyes, think about his posture, think about the tone of his voice. To want something—no, to *need* something so badly from the only One who can give it—is a place of vulnerability and desperation. We need to be there.

40. Everything seems to change in verse 50. What phrase sticks out to you from that verse? Why?

41. Verses 51 through 53 are confirmation of the timing of the miracle. The nobleman left Jesus not knowing anything for sure. In fact, it took him a while to get home (verse 52). What emotions would the servants have been experiencing over that same period?

42. Because this nobleman went to find Jesus, many were affected. List everyone from this account who was touched in some way by this man's faith and cite how that person was changed.

But to You I have cried out, Oh Lord, and in the
morning my prayer comes before You.
—Psalm 88:13

JOHN CHAPTER 5

Marketing companies charge a lot of money to think of ways to get us to spend our money. Finding, developing, and tapping into our motivations to purchase is big business. I have noticed that in advertising, fear can be a major tool of choice to sway me. Buy this toothpaste so you won't have cavities. Pack a fun lunch so your kids will have friends. Get a security system so you won't be a victim.

What is my motivation for the actions and decisions I make throughout the day? To be honest, most of the time, I don't consciously think about it. I can go about my day and never once have it cross my mind to wonder *why* I'm doing what I'm doing. It takes effort to think on such things and time—it does take time. I'm too busy to think of why I chose to turn left rather than right, why I took the fries rather than the coleslaw, or why I said, "No, thank you" to the offer of "Is there anything else I can do for you today?"

We begin chapter five with another account of physical healing, but in this one Jesus asks a question that, on its surface, appears ridiculous given the circumstances. It is a question, however, that we all need to ask ourselves when we are serious about letting the Lord move us forward in our walks with Him.

READ JOHN 5:1–15

1. Although verse 1 states "there was a feast of the Jews," it does not specify which feast. The occasion does explain why Jesus was in Jerusalem, however. What does it tell us about Jesus that He would pay attention to such things?

2. John gives very specific details about the site of this miracle. From verse 2, write all the particulars he gives us.

3. At this point, we know *when* and we know *where*. In verse 3, we find out *who* ("a great multitude of sick people"). To continue our thought, according to verse 3, *why* were they there?

We can appreciate John's commentary in verse 4 because otherwise we wouldn't know why they were waiting. It probably doesn't really matter if there was solid evidence that this healing occurred on a regular basis or if it ever happened at all.

- Maybe one time someone happened to get into the water while it was stirring and he or she felt differently upon exiting.
- Maybe an angel really did stir the water. We know that spiritual forces were certainly active at the time of Jesus.
- In reality, being the first to step into the water could be a very difficult thing to discern in a crowd, and being made well could be hard to define.

The bottom line is this: desperate people believe desperate things. We know that. We will search and cling to every bit of hope we can muster in an otherwise hopeless situation.

4. In verse 5, we meet a man, a specific man in a crowd of people (remember "a great multitude of sick people"). Write what we either know about him or what we can discern about him from this entire passage.

Thirty-eight years is a long period of time. As a point of reference, thirty-eight years from the time of this writing was 1983. Here are some of the things happening in 1983.

- Gas was selling at $1.16 per gallon
- The average income per year was $24,580
- Sally Ride became the first American woman in space on the space shuttle Challenger
- Microsoft Word was first released
- McDonalds introduced the McNugget
- President Ronald Reagan made his initial proposal to develop technology to intercept enemy missiles. The media calls this plan "Star Wars."
- *Star Wars VI: The Return of the Jedi* was released in theaters
- Most TV viewers only had four channels from which to choose. The Fox Channel didn't premier until 1985 and cable was still in its infancy.

You get the point. It's a long time.

5. What are some of the things that would or could happen to a person's mindset who has been sick for thirty-eight years?

Optional: Do some research on what physically happens to the body after not walking for thirty-eight years and write your findings here.

6. The fact that Jesus asks the question in verse 6 would suggest that the man may have had another motivation for being at the pool that morning. If not for healing, why on earth would he be there?

7. Jesus knows every thought before we think it and He knew all about this man, too. Why would He ask him this question?

8. What are your impressions of the man's reply in verse 7?

Most likely, this man was meeting Jesus face to face for the first time. He didn't know Him. He didn't know what He could do. It is understandable that he had excuses for Jesus, but what about me.

What is my reply to my Lord when He says to me

- "Do you want to be made well?"
- "Do you want to change your attitude?"
- "Do you want to forgive that person?"
- "Do you want to fix that relationship?"

9. Jesus gives him three commands. What are they (verse 8)?

10. Prior to those words, the man could not do any of those things. Think of it: seconds before Jesus spoke, the man's world looked one way and then, *bam*, it looked like something else. Read verse 9 and think through what the Lord had given the man. Write your thoughts.

11. There is immediate opposition. Incredible. What do you think the motivation was for the crowd response in verse 10?

Note that "the Jews" refers to the Jewish leaders, not everyone in Israel.

The man has no answer except his testimony of what Jesus had just done for him (verse 11). All of a sudden, this guy was the center of attention in a sea of people. Our Jesus sees us in the crowd. He sees our needs. He sees our hurts. In fact, He sees us before we even know or acknowledge who He is (verse 13).

12. Jesus has one more conversation with the man after finding him in the temple (verse 14). Why do you think that is the first place the man went?

13. The man went back and cleared up the question of "Who is the man?" with his interrogators (verse 15). To keep with our theme, we will address the question of motivation once more. What could have been his reasoning for making the effort to find "the Jews" again?

READ JOHN 5:16–23

14. From verses 16 through 18, list all the reasons the Jews sought to kill Jesus.

15. John uses very strong language in these verses regarding the intent of Jesus's pursuers. At this point, His public ministry had not been going on that long. Why did Jesus elicit such passionate feelings relatively early on?

16. How we view Jesus is a reflection of how we view God. Make a list of everything that Jesus says about Himself from verses 19 through 23.

We have plenty in the above list to see that Jesus is claiming to be equal with God. At this time, in this crowd, this claim would evoke very emotional and passionate responses, but this is the time and the place the Lord chose.

17. Because of its importance, we will revisit this question throughout this study. Why is it crucial that we know and believe that Jesus is God?

READ JOHN 5:24–30

Jesus goes on to address the crowd as they continue to be more agitated and probably more hostile. He was not mincing words. His ministry years were short on Earth. There was urgency when He spoke because the eternity of every soul in the crowd was at stake.

18. In the Jewish mindset, "hearing" and "obeying" went hand in hand. If you did not "obey," you could not imply that you "heard." When Jesus says "he who hears my word," what "word" is He referring to (verse 24)?

19. "Shall not come into judgment" (verse 24). What should terrify us about any kind of *judgment*?

20. Sometimes in our hearts and minds, we aren't scared of being judged. Why?

21. Having a healthy fear of the final judgment is good because that will lead us to the truth of our incredible lack. Any other conclusion we come to is a pride that will lead us straight to hell. However, Jesus is our righteous judge and he has graciously given us an invitation to know Him. Three times in these seven verses, Jesus says He will judge or refers to His judgment. List a few other places in the New Testament where Jesus is referred to in this way as being the final judge.

READ JOHN 5:31–47

22. In verse 31, Jesus refers to a principle with which they would have been familiar. Look at Deuteronomy 19:15 and summarize in your own words what it says.

23. Basically, Jesus says, "You don't have to believe who I am because I'm saying it. I have three witnesses who will say the same thing." From verses 32 through 37, list the three.

1)

2)

3)

24. Write what Jesus says of John the Baptist (verse 35).

25. Write what Jesus says of His works (verse 36).

26. Write what Jesus says of the Father (verses 37–38).

27. Verses 39 and 40 are some of the saddest in all the book of John because they (remember, it's the *crowds* He is talking to) *thought* they had the answers. They *thought* they were doing it right. "Thinking they knew" was keeping them from seeing Jesus. What are some other things (or thoughts) that can keep us from seeing who He really is?

We can probably surmise that some in the crowd must have thought He was reading their minds. How could He be saying, "You do not have the love of God in you"? Why would He say it? Weren't they doing the right things? Weren't they reading the right things?

After spending time with Jesus, often self-examination needs to take place. Many times, He will challenge us with His words. By bringing up the name of Moses (verses 45–47), He is referring to their history—a history that they had great pride in. They knew the writings of Moses (many males in the crowd undoubtedly had memorized the entire Torah [the first five books of the Old Testament written by Moses] during their first few years of formal education). To hear this man say he (Moses) "wrote about Me" was something perplexing.

28. Cite a few examples where Moses wrote about Jesus in the first five books of the Old Testament. (I'll get you started with Numbers 21:8–9.)

29. Has your personal time with Jesus ever resulted in a reshaping of something you thought you knew? If so, share it here.

Let the words of my mouth and the meditation of my heart be
acceptable in Your sight, O Lord, my strength and my Redeemer.
—PSALM 19:14

JOHN CHAPTER 6

This chapter is the longest in the book of John with seventy-one verses. There is a lot of information packed in, as you can imagine, but we will focus on this question: When you are near Jesus, you will

1) *See* some amazing things and 2) *hear* some challenging things.

What will you and I do with the information we take in from being close to Him? By the end of this chapter, many who saw and heard had chosen to leave.

To *see* Jesus, to *hear* Jesus—crowds would gather in throngs to catch a glimpse of what He would do. In a time when there was no sound amplification except the natural landscape, people would sit on the grass for hours and listen to Him teach. They were families and individuals. They were the elderly and the children. They were the healthy and the sick. They were the lonely and the broken. They were the curious and they were the skeptical.

However, drawing numbers was not the Lord's goal. Popularity does not equal success. It is the heart of the *one* that always presses upon the heart of Jesus. He saw each one in the crowd of thousands and He sees you and me today.

Now it becomes personal because I'm forced to answer for the things that I see and hear. How do His actions affect me? How do His words move me? Do I really desire to see what He wants to show me or hear what He has to say to me?

A note of caution: on the surface, since we are engaged in a Bible study, it would seem that all of us could say "yes" to that last question. Like the man at the pool, do I really *want* to be made well personally? What Jesus meant to the crowds is one thing, but when He captures the heart of the one who is truly seeking, it is a completely different life-changing thing altogether.

READ JOHN 6:1

1. In 6:1, the phrase "after these things" takes on new meaning when you read the account in Matthew and Mark. Look at Matthew 14:1–12 and Mark 6:14–29 and write a summary of what had just happened prior to this miracle in John 6:1–14.

2. In thinking about the relationship between Jesus and John the Baptist, how do you think this would have affected Him?

This is our backdrop for one of Jesus's most memorable miracles. The feeding of the 5,000 was recorded in each of the gospels and we will be looking at all four accounts to take in all the information available to us on this event. In order to do this, you might be tempted to cut corners and skim over each as it will take a bit of effort to get through all four at once. I would encourage you to fight against that urge and take your time with each passage of Scripture documenting this miracle.

3. Let's start by reading through each account once. Read Matthew 14:13–21, Mark 6:30–44, Luke 9:10–17, and John 6:1–14.

4. For each of the sections below, list any similarities or differences.

	Similarities	Differences
Matthew 14:13–14		
Mark 6:31–34		
Luke 9:10–11		
John 6:1–4		

Matthew 14:15–16		
Mark 6:35–37		
Luke 9:12		
John 6:5–7		

Matthew 14:17–19		
Mark 6:38–41		
Luke 9:13–16		
John 6:8–11		

Matthew 14:20–21

Mark 6:42–44

Luke 9:17

John 6:12–14

---

5. Although looking at all the accounts at once fills in a lot of detail for us, there are still some things we have no idea about this side of heaven. List some questions you would love to have answers to. (For example, did the people farthest from Jesus know where the food came from?)

Some might consider the above question silly or childish, but the heart behind it is to put us in a place where the account is more than just a story we may have heard in a children's class many times. Jesus placed Himself outside of time and produced bread while skipping all the processes that would normally be required. He created mature fish that were ready to be eaten immediately. The miracle is not only the number of people He fed with such a small amount, but also the way He chose to do it.

6. What is a practical truth you can take away personally from this miracle?

The disciples definitely had seen an amazing thing that day, but Jesus wasn't quite done with what He wanted them to see.

READ JOHN 6:15–21

7. Why was the crowd ready to make Him a king?

8. Yet, Jesus "departed." Why (verse 15)?

9. Matthew 14:22 tells us that, "Jesus made His disciples get into the boat and go before Him on the other side." Why is this point significant when looking at the whole account?

10. The Sea of Galilee is low-lying and surrounded by hills, making it susceptible to violent windstorms. It is approximately 157 feet deep at its maximum depth,[10] which is also a factor in sudden wind gusts whipping up the water. However, these were men familiar with this body of water. Many of the group had spent their lives in this place. Why do you think Jesus brought them here to witness His next miracle?

---

[10] "Sea of Galilee," Britannica, accessed April 18, 2023, https://www.britannica.com/place/Sea-of-Galilee.

11. Tucked in the middle of verse 19 is the miraculous event that Jesus allowed His disciples to see. Place yourself in that boat. The circumstances themselves were enough to make it a fearful situation. It was dark, the wind was blowing, the waves were high and then…there was Jesus. List everything He does in verses 19 through 21.

12. Read the account in Mark 6:45–52 and list any details not included in John's narrative.

Of note, John does not mention anything about Peter walking on water during this occurrence. You can read about that in Matthew 14:22–33, if you like.

13. Many times, the Lord will allow challenges in an area where we have felt very comfortable in the past (such as the middle of the Sea of Galilee for the disciples). Why do you think He sometimes chooses this for us?

Oh, taste and see that the Lord is good, Blessed is the man who trusts in Him.
—PSALM 34:8

READ JOHN 6:22–40

Verses 22 through 24 paint a picture for us of the scene that lay before John the morning after these two miraculous events. The remainder of the chapter will focus around what Jesus *said* to the crowds as opposed to what He *showed* them.

14. The people who were left at this point had stayed in the area overnight. What do you think were some of the reasons they were motivated to "seek Jesus" that morning (verse 24)?

15. Rather than answering their question in verse 25, Jesus got to the heart of their presence there. Why does He say they were "seeking" Him (verse 26)?

16. What should they have been looking for (verse 27)?

17. Laboring for things that will ultimately perish is still so common today, even for believers. What are some examples of that in our day?

18. The crowds posed a question to Jesus and we should all be very interested in hearing the answer. There are many who populate churches who want to live by a list of dos and don'ts. From verse 29, what is Jesus's answer to the question in verse 28?

19. If "belief" is the work, what does that look like in my everyday Christian life? How do I know I'm pleasing God?

Yet, they wanted to *see* more. We get that. Our senses cry out to be satisfied with some kind of explanation that seems reasonable—something that connects the dots of our faith. Faith by itself seems like it's not enough somehow.

> See, I know about the manna.
> I know what I've always heard about the manna.
> I know what happened in the wilderness.
> But Jesus says, "Wait a second…rethink what you think you know."

20. What is the difference between manna and the "bread from heaven" that Jesus is speaking of in verse 32?

21. By calling Himself the "bread of life," what is Jesus saying?

22. Everything that Jesus did or said ultimately was about God's will. According to verse 40, what is His will?

READ JOHN 6:41–59

23. The word translated as "complained" in verse 41 literally means "to murmur, mutter, grumble, to say anything against in a low tone."[11] They were displeased with what they were hearing from Him, but not shouting at Jesus or His disciples. They were murmuring, grumbling among themselves. What kind of damage is done when this is our habit?

24. Jesus answers them in verses 44 through 51. Let's remember that Jesus didn't teach like anyone else. He taught with authority (Matt. 7:29 and Mark 1:22), so it must have been confusing when He said things that seemed to go against what they thought they knew about God or about Him. Look through Jesus's reply and make a list of everything He says about Himself in these eight verses.

There's little doubt that verse 51 was the most controversial to the audience, but it was going to get worse in verses 53 through 57—and He said all this in the synagogue (verse 59). Think back on what the crowd had just seen the day before from the man who is saying these things. We can almost be certain that this was not what they were expecting.

25. At this point in the narrative, what do you think were the disciples' reactions to all this, inwardly and/or outwardly?

---

[11] "G1111 - gongyzō - Strong's Greek Lexicon (nkjv)." Blue Letter Bible. Accessed 29 May, 2023. https://www.blueletterbible.org/lexicon/g1111/nkjv/tr/0-1/

26. Jesus makes it clear in verse 63 that the things He had just said were not literal. What did He mean in verse 56?

READ JOHN 6:60–71

The scene is quite compelling. People were leaving. When Jesus says hard things, there are choices to be made. Each individual must decide for himself or herself.

27. The word "disciple" in verse 60 simply means "learner." These were more than the twelve (the Apostles will be addressed separately beginning in verse 67). While they had not been part of Jesus's close circle, they had distinguished themselves as being different from the throngs that followed Him. For this group, their choice was now verse 66. If asked, what do you think their reasoning would be for walking away?

28. People who would consider themselves "learners" occupy chairs in churches all the time, until something is said that causes them to drift away. What should be the response from those who stay? Use Scripture to back up your answer.

29. In the end, every one of us has to come to a place where we can say for ourselves, "Lord, to whom shall we go? You have the words of eternal life" (verse 68). What are some things that we need to do before we hear the difficult things to insure that our hearts can handle them correctly?

Jesus answered and said to them, "This is the work of God, that you believe in Him whom He sent."
—JOHN 6:29

JOHN CHAPTER 7

This chapter also starts with the phrase "After these things." Chapter 6 started this same way. One of the benefits of dissecting the Word of God is that we know what "things" John was referring to, at least in part. As the days and months of Jesus's ministry passed, the crowds reacted, individuals reacted, and John was paying attention.

The religious leadership thought they knew Jesus, but they also thought they knew what the Messiah would be like, and therein was the conflict for the majority of them. His brothers, too, had their own opinions about what He should and shouldn't do. Chapter 7 is full of misconceptions and wrong conclusions. He divided the crowds, which was precisely what He came to do (Luke 12:51).

READ JOHN 7:1–24

1. Look back at John 5:18 and write why "the Jews sought to kill Him."

2. We are now entering the last six months of Jesus's ministry. The accusations are getting louder and the discussions more heated. From verses 3 through 4, what did His brothers want Him to do?

3. Belief was not their motivation (verse 5), so what do you think was their reason for urging Him to go to the Feast?

4. It's interesting to me that John records this conversation between Jesus and His brothers because we find out in verse 10 that Jesus *does* attend the feast. Why do you think Jesus responded the way He did to them in verse 8?

5. Belief in Jesus is not about physical closeness, as evidenced by the disbelief of the brothers who grew up in the same household. Belief in Jesus is an issue of the heart, then and now. People can come to church every Sunday and Wednesday and still be unbelievers. After the resurrection, there will be a change in His brothers (Acts 1:14). What is the change that has to happen in the heart of every believer?

6. In general, why is something done "in secret"?

7. Why do you think Jesus went to the feast "in secret" (verse 10)?

8. The Jews expected Him to be there. They knew He'd be there. What were some things that they knew about Jesus that would lead them to believe He would be at this feast in Jerusalem?

9. He knew that the Jews "sought to kill Him" and yet, what was He doing in verse 14?

The religious authority (the Jews) "marveled" at His teaching. The word *marvel* means "to wonder, to be in awe of."[12] They could not figure Him out. There were miracles. There was teaching. There was kindness. There was anger. Who was this man?

10. What is the dictionary definition of *doctrine*?

11. According to verses 16 through 18, what makes doctrine important?

Before going any further, let's take a brief look at the Feast of Tabernacles. Read Leviticus 23:33–44, then Deuteronomy 16:13–17, and finally Deuteronomy 31:9–13. These people loved their history and they loved the law. The events of John chapter 7 occur during this feast. Days of national celebration are ways to mark time. In the United States, we have

---

[12] "G2296 - thaumazō - Strong's Greek Lexicon (nkjv)." Blue Letter Bible. Accessed 29 May, 2023. https://www.blueletterbible.org/lexicon/g2296/nkjv/tr/0-1/

Thanksgiving and the Fourth of July, for example. Place yourself in the mindset of the masses of people who were gathered in Jerusalem at this time. The sights and sounds for this feast would have been predictable and familiar—but then there was Jesus.

12. By pointing out their hypocrisy in verse 23, Jesus asks them to rethink everything they thought they knew. How does a person judge with "righteous judgment"? What is it and how is it acquired?

READ JOHN 7:25–31

Throughout this chapter, John places us in the middle of a crowd where we can hear the conversations first hand. In this section, it is clear that there are those who are aware of the talk of killing Jesus (as opposed to those in verse 20). In fact, not only is there talk of it, but about which group is doing the talking.

13. In your own words, what was this group "from Jerusalem" accusing their rulers of exactly (verses 25–26)?

14. There was a tradition in their day that the Messiah would appear out of nowhere, surrounded by mystery (verse 27). Old Testament prophecy, however, told a much different story. List three or four prophecies from the Old Testament that were directly fulfilled by Jesus's birth.

15. It is an amazing scene in the temple as Jesus plainly stated who He was (verses 28–29). His words were challenging to the hearers. What was He saying about Himself?

16. Many believed in Him because of what they saw Him do (verse 31). In that respect, He *did* meet their expectations of the Messiah. List some things about Jesus that definitely did not fit what many in Israel had in mind for "the Christ."

READ JOHN 7:32–36

17. You can almost feel the tension mounting as you read this section of Scripture. The religious leadership of the day was becoming very frustrated with Jesus. His teachings called so many things into question that had always been understood. What do you think they were they hoping to accomplish by capturing Him (verse 32)?

18. Below is a list of three groups of people who are present to hear Jesus's words in verses 33 and 34. For each group, write out their motive for seeking Him and what their concerns might be for not being able to find Him.

Religious leaders:

The crowd:

The disciples:

19. Whatever the motive, His words so resonated in their minds they asked, "What is this thing that He said" (verse 36). Why do you think John included this observation for us?

READ JOHN 7:37–44

> "The Feast of Tabernacles lasted eight days. All through the first seven days water from the Pool of Siloam was carried in a golden pitcher and poured out at the altar to remind everyone of the water God miraculously provided for a thirsty Israel in the wilderness. It seems that on the eighth day there was *no* pouring of water — only prayers for water — to remind them that they came into the Promised Land."[13]

The above information adds to the scene of verse 37. John intends to paint a picture for us. The crowds had seen the High Priest and the water and the pitcher every day for seven days. Then Jesus stood and cried out.

---

[13] Guzik, D. "Study Guide for John 7 by David Guzik." Blue Letter Bible. Last Modified 6/2022. https://www. blueletterbible.org/comm/guzik_david/study-guide/john/john-7.cfm

20. Everyone thirsts for water (we must have it to live), but what is Jesus referring to in verse 37? What need is He going to satisfy when we come to Him?

John actually provides commentary on verse 38 with verse 39. At the time Jesus spoke the words "out of his heart will flow rivers of living water," John probably did not know exactly what He was referring to. As he penned his gospel, the Holy Spirit Himself gave John the insight to let us know what our Lord meant.

21. In the life of the believer, what does it look like in a practical sense to have the Holy Spirit flowing out from the heart?

22. John states that the Holy Spirit had not yet been given when Jesus spoke the words of verses 37 and 38. When was the Holy Spirit given?

23. Write out Luke 12:51.

24. The above verse and John 7:43 are the reality of Jesus in the days He walked this earth. They are every bit as true today. Why does He divide?

25. List a few examples in our culture where the name of Jesus has divided when other religions are placated.

26. With all the crowds in Jerusalem for the feast, there must have been ample opportunity to detain Him. Why did "no one" lay a hand on Him" (verse 44)?

READ JOHN 7:45–52

Once again, John has us "overhearing" a conversation in the crowd. This time the religious leadership is questioning why their orders have not been carried out.

27. Why were the chief priests and Pharisees anxious to have this matter taken care of?

28. There is much pride represented in the verses of this section. They were zealous, but not for the right things. In their zeal, they missed Jesus Himself right in front of them. Their hearts were becoming increasingly hardened. What were they doing (or not doing) that was accelerating their hatred towards Jesus?

29. Of course, there was Nicodemus (verse 50). We know him from chapter 3. Why do you think John records his statement in verse 51?

30. One of the warnings, I believe, in chapter 7 is that we need to be careful what we "think" we know. My mind can be so focused on something I perceive as "fact," that I will miss the opportunity for the Lord to show me what is *actually* correct. As believers, what are practical things we can do to keep this from happening individually?

The Lord will guide you continually,
And satisfy your soul in drought,
And strengthen your bones;
You shall be like a watered garden,
And like a spring of water, whose waters do not fail.
—ISAIAH 58:11

JOHN CHAPTER 8

This chapter is full of conflict (once again) between Jesus and the religious leadership of His day. They were constantly watching His every move and questioning His every word. These men were seen as representing God Himself to the people. There was a certain status involved in knowing and "keeping" all the law. There was a prestige in people making certain assumptions about their motives. It was a lot to live up to, but it was even greater to think about giving it all up.

There is a saying, "knowledge is power," but the real power is in knowing the *right* things and applying those things *correctly*. When Jesus came, it was hard for the scribes and Pharisees to see past their expectations of what the Messiah was going to be and do. Since they were "supposed" to know, it also became difficult for the people to ascertain the truth.

It boils down to this. There is no substitute for a personal encounter with Jesus. The law can bring you to Him, but then it has to leave you there so He can do the rest. No matter how we get there, our stories need to end at the feet of Jesus.

READ JOHN 7:53–8:12

1. From verse 8:1 alone, we cannot conclude that Jesus went often to the Mount of Olives. Take a look at Luke 21:37 and Luke 22:39. What can we say fairly confidently about this place?

2. What are some of your thoughts on why He might have loved this place?

I don't know what the routine and rhythm of Jerusalem would have looked like before Jesus began his public ministry. However, if we look at where we are in John 8, it appears that the crowds and religious leaders were fixated on Jesus and His teaching now that He was on the scene, from early in the morning until late at night.

3. What was happening in verse 2?

4. Read verse 3 and try to get a visual of this scene in your mind. What are your thoughts, feelings, and/or impressions about what has just happened?

5. Read Leviticus 20:10 and Deuteronomy 17:2–7. Why do you think the punishment was so great for adultery in Israel?

6. It was a serious matter to be caught in this sin, but it was also very serious to bring the accusation because you needed to be prepared to "throw the first stone" (Deut. 17:7). Why was this one of the safeguards in bringing this allegation?

7. Verse 6 tells us the motivation of the scribes and Pharisees in this matter. How would this have "tested" Jesus?

8. There are different schools of thought on what Jesus was writing on the ground in verse 6. Maybe it was the sins of her accusers, maybe it was the Law in order to remind them of the Ten Commandments, or maybe He just doodled. Ultimately, it doesn't matter because if it did, the Holy Spirit would have included that detail for us. Why do you think He chose to act "as though He did not hear" (verse 6)?

9. In His response in verse 7, He referred to Deuteronomy 17:7. They may have thought they would be saved from this portion of the law since they were in a group. We will often do things in a group that we would never do individually. What are some reasons for this?

10. As a result of the Lord's question and His delay in answering the accusation about the woman, what happens in verse 9?

11. It is now about Jesus and the woman alone. Had her accusers stayed, what would they have seen (verses 10–11)?

12. What is one thing that stands out for you about Jesus from this account?

READ JOHN 8:13–20

13. One of the things that we are told of Jesus's teaching is that He spoke with "authority" (Luke 4:32). That did not mean that the Pharisees did not take every opportunity to challenge what He said. What is their challenge to Him in this section of Scripture?

14. By skimming through this section, write the reasons Jesus gives for His testimony about Himself being true.

15. Why do you think John included the fact that He spoke these things in the "treasury" (verse 20)?

READ JOHN 8:21–30

16. In verse 24, Jesus states that those who do not "believe that I am He" will die in their sins, but many did believe. Each of the following verses contains the phrase "many believed." Read a bit of the context of each and write *why* they believed.

John 2:23:

John 8:30:

John 10:42:

John 12:42:

17. The word "believed" in verse 30 is *pisteuo* in the Greek, which means "to be persuaded of, to place confidence in."[14] What exactly are we "placing our confidence in" when we believe in Jesus?

---

[14] "G4100 - pisteuō - Strong's Greek Lexicon (kjv)." Blue Letter Bible. Accessed 29 May, 2023. https://www.blueletterbible.org/lexicon/g4100/kjv/tr/0-1/

READ JOHN 8:31–36

18. Note that Jesus is speaking to believers now in verse 31 when He says, "If you abide in My word." What does that mean to us practically?

19. Why is "slave to sin" such an appropriate description of those committing habitual sin (verse 34)?

20. A life that is free is available to all believers, but why is it that some do not live like they are free (verse 36)?

Stand fast therefore in the liberty by which Christ has made us free and do not be entangled again with a yoke of bondage.
—GALATIANS 5:1

READ JOHN 8:37–47

21. What are the "works of Abraham" that Jesus refers to in verse 39? Give Scripture to back up your answer.

22. Jesus is very blunt in this passage. As you go back through these verses, choose one statement of Jesus's that you think the heaviest. Write the reference for it here and include why you think He spoke in such a manner.

23. The ears of the crowd were working, so when He says, "You do not hear," what does Jesus mean (verse 47)?

READ JOHN 8:48–59

24. Why were the crowds so incensed when Jesus mentioned Abraham?

25. Why do you think He chose to mention Abraham so often?

26. Write out verse 58 here. Simply amazing.

Now when He had said to them "I am He," they
drew back and fell to the ground.
—JOHN 18:6

JOHN CHAPTER 9

The apostle John spends all of chapter 9 documenting a healing that took place on a Sabbath. In fact, it's the entire picture of the scene from beginning to end. We don't have every detail, but we have enough to give us a snapshot of what happened during this short few moments or hours of Jesus's encounter with this man, this recipient of God's gift of healing, this unnamed beneficiary of God's mercy.

It's interesting to me that none of the other gospels mention this particular miracle. Maybe it's not so much that they don't include the event as it is that John spends one whole chapter on it in a book that only has twenty-one chapters in total. This was significant to John. This one stood out.

John might have been a fisherman by trade, but the Holy Spirit made him an observer and a writer to bring this account to life.

We'll begin by reading the entire chapter.

READ JOHN 9

1. There are things that make this an extraordinary miracle (as if there are any other kindJ). Verse 1 cites our first: this man was "blind from birth." Do not make the mistake of passing over that fact too quickly? If you do, you will miss how very personal this account really is. List some things that he would have never experienced because he was born blind.

2. We don't know how old he was when he met Jesus, but he is labeled "a man," so he's not a child. If the question in verse 2 is *voiced* by the disciples, we can be certain that others in town had *thought* the same thing over the years. We are always looking for a reason something happens. Why do you think we do this?

3. Jesus gives the disciples (and us) the very reason in verse 3. Write it here.

4. If you and I applied this truth to every hard circumstance in our lives, how would that change our mindsets?

5. Sometimes sin (either ours or someone else's) *is* the reason for our difficulties, but the truth of what God can do is still very applicable. Write at least three references from Scripture that would encourage us in this hope.

6. When Jesus says, "I am the light of the world" (verse 5), what is He here to illuminate exactly?

The people who walked in darkness have seen a great light.
—ISAIAH 9:2A

7. The man did not ask for healing, yet healing is exactly what Jesus gave him. He received an amazing gift from our Lord by simply following the instructions he was given (verse 7). What do you think the man would have known of Jesus at this point?

8. In order to receive his sight, what did he have to do?

9. He had to physically "go and wash," but there was nothing magical about the place or the act. What healed this man?

Sometimes Jesus will restore something we had, but there are times when He will give us something completely new. This man had never been able to see—never. He saw no green grass, no blue sky, no parents' faces; he saw nothing but darkness.

I'm sure he knew he wasn't like other people, but he couldn't have fathomed how his life was going to change forever. For the remainder of his days on this earth, he was "that guy:" the guy who was born blind, and then met Jesus and "came back seeing" (verse 7).

10. What does this mean practically for you personally right now?

"Daughter, your faith has made you well."
—MARK 5:34

11. As the man comes back, there seems to be some controversy as to who he really is. This is rather absurd because this man was part of the community. The text even specifies those who questioned him were "neighbors and those who had previously seen that he was blind" (verse 8). Why do you think there was any talk at all of his identity?

12. Upon establishing (and confirming) who he was, then came the big question: what happened to him (verse 10)? The man's reply in verse 11 is wonderfully simple. Sometimes when we tell (or retell) a story, we include details that are unnecessary (maybe in an effort to make it more interesting). There was certainly none of that in verse 11. At this point, what did he know about Jesus?

13. Read each of the following passages and write a brief summary of each.

Mark 8:22–25

Luke 18:35–43

14. Our Jesus will not be "put in a box." We cannot predict how, when, or why He works. What are your thoughts on this statement?

15. Now the Pharisees enter our account. John records for us that this healing took place on the Sabbath (verse 14). Why do you think he felt that worthy of note?

16. The man told the same story to this group as he had to the first (verse 15) but the Pharisees' reaction is to question the character of the healer Himself. For them, the two thoughts of being "from God" and "keeping the Sabbath" were inseparable. Take a look at the following verses: Exodus 31:14, Exodus 31:16, and Deuteronomy 5:15. After reading these three verses, write some reasons the Pharisees held the Sabbath in such high regard.

17. By healing on the Sabbath, what do you think Jesus was trying to show them?

18. In verses 18 through 23, the man's parents become involved. What a day it had been for them! From this passage, make a list of things they could confirm for the Jews.

19. They were not ready to confirm *who* did the healing. What was their reason (verse 22)?

20. Fear is a great motivator and a very effective tool the enemy uses to hold us back. What might be examples of the modern-day equivalent for being "put out of the synagogue" for us?

21. In verses 24 through 34, they continue to chide the man on what had happened to him and he is becoming understandably agitated. In rereading verses 24 through 29, how would you describe the attitude of the healed man?

22. Why do you think the religious leaders pressed him so hard? What were they looking for?

23. There is a lot of truth crammed in verses 30 through 33. This truth was being proclaimed by a man as a result of one personal encounter with Jesus and *not* by the Pharisees (the "most religious" people of the time). What phrase from this short testimony of the man who was healed sticks out most to you personally and why?

24. It is easy to read over the phrase "they cast him out" and miss the personal nature of the consequences. Think through and list some ways you think this would have affected his everyday life.

Then there is Jesus.

The man had received his sight, but now Jesus was about to put all the pieces together for him to change his eternity.

25. These things were revealed to the man *after* he was "cast out." What are some of the practical applications of this?

26. How does the man respond to who Jesus is (verse 38)?

27. What causes you personally to respond in worship to our Lord?

"For the Son of Man has come to seek and save that which was lost."
—Luke 19:10

JOHN CHAPTER 10

This chapter is about shepherds and sheep. John will document for us what Jesus had to say about the behavior of both. Before reading the chapter, we might as well get comfortable with the premise that we are sheep. Several times in the Old and New Testaments, we are characterized as such, but this is the first time Jesus refers to Himself as the Shepherd. Picturing Jesus as our Shepherd changes the entire analogy for the believer because now, we can begin to see our practical needs as sheep and His practical provision as our Shepherd.

Below is a short list of facts about sheep taken from the website www.sheep101.info. The list can be beneficial in our understanding as to why we are called "sheep" throughout the entire Bible. I do not believe that the Lord made sheep stupid, just desperately dependent on the shepherd.

- **Flocking behavior**. Sheep have a strong flocking (herding) and following instinct. If something frightens them, they band together in large groups. This is really their only protection from predators.
- **Follow the leader.** When one sheep moves, all of the others will follow (sometimes to their detriment). From birth, a lamb is taught to follow the older members of the flock.
- **Social.** Sheep are very social. While eating, they need to see the other sheep. This is essential in keeping them calm. A sheep singled out from the rest will become stressed and agitated.
- **Normal sheep behavior.** Sheep are so predictable in behavior that changes in such can be a huge indicator of their overall health. Isolation from the rest of the flock, lack of appetite, and inactivity are most likely signs of an unhealthy sheep.[15]

---

[15] Schoenian, Susan. "Basic Sheep Info." Sheep101.info. Last modified 4/2021. Accessed May 29, 2023. http://www.sheep101.info/bahavior.html

READ JOHN 10:1–6

1. Although the sheep have a shepherd, it is clear from this section that there are others trying to get at the sheep. Make a list from these verses of characteristics of the true shepherd.

2. If we use this picture as Jesus intended, seeing believers as the sheep and Himself as the Shepherd, take each characteristic you have listed above and write how each applies to Jesus.

3. Why do you think they didn't understand (verse 6)?

READ JOHN 10:7–21

4. What is the purpose of a door? (Don't overthink it. Just write a simple explanation.)

5. Jesus calls Himself the "door" in verses 7 and 9. What is He keeping in and what is He keeping out?

6. How does a nonbeliever get in?

7. What does the phrase "life more abundant" mean (verse 10)?

8. Jesus says He came to give this kind of life to every believer, but there are many who would not describe their lives in this way. What are some roadblocks to living life "abundantly"?

9. To help us grasp the depth of the word "good" when used to describe our "good Shepherd," Jesus uses compare and contrast with a "hireling" (verse 12). The hireling is different than those described in verse 8. Unlike the thief and robber, a hireling's motive is not clear until there is a threat present. Why is a hireling especially dangerous to the sheep?

10. Pastors are referred to as under-shepherds as they serve the people they have been entrusted with under the Good Shepherd. What are some verses/passages that give us the basis for this title of under-shepherd?

11. How can verses 11 through 15 be applied practically to the local pastor?

12. The "other sheep" in verse 16 are Gentile believers (not of Jewish decent). In referring to this group, Jesus says, "Them also I must bring." List at least one other place in the gospels where Jesus makes it clear that He came to save all people, not just the Jews.

13. Once again, John mentions that there was division among the people because of Jesus (verse 19). Of His statements in verses 17 and 18, which do you think was the most controversial to the crowd at this time and why?

14. John not only tells us about the division Jesus was causing, but he also records what some of the people were saying about Him (verses 20–21). Many things could be said of Jesus, but there was no escaping the fact that they had just seen a man who was blind from birth begin to see. What do you think were some of the reasons the crowds continued to follow Him around?

READ JOHN 10:22–30

Most commentators believe that there was a passage of time between verses 21 and 22, maybe as much as two and a half months. The Feast of Dedication was a celebration instituted by Judas Maccabeus in 164 BC. The feast commemorates the rededication of the temple after three years of desecration by the Romans. This time of national celebration is marked by lots of light and joy. The city of Jerusalem was illuminated both in its structure and in the people's hearts.

15. It was against this backdrop of national pride that "the Jews" inquired impatiently of Jesus. What do they ask Him in verse 24?

16. There is no doubt that some in the crowd had been present a few months earlier and heard Him speak of shepherds and sheep. What does Jesus offer to the "sheep" that hear His voice (verses 27–29)?

17. They asked Him to speak "plainly," and He could not be more clear than in verse 30. What is Jesus saying about Himself by making this statement?

READ JOHN 10:31–39

18. It is not difficult to work a crowd into a frenzy. The "mob mentality" can take over relatively quickly in a heated situation. In general, why is this a dangerous situation in which to find ourselves no matter which "side" we are on?

19. Look at Leviticus 24:16. I am certain that some in this crowd genuinely thought they were doing the right thing in taking up stones. Have you ever been so focused on what you thought was right and then found out later you were wrong?

20. As you scan these eight verses, make note of Jesus's reaction to this crowd. Think through what He *could* have said or *could* have done. Remember the power He possessed. Write your thoughts here.

READ JOHN 10:40–42

After all the turmoil, these verses are somewhat of a rest from all that has just happened. We are getting very close to Jesus's final week before His crucifixion. He knew well of the suffering that was approaching quickly.

21. Write out verse 42.

"O Jerusalem, Jerusalem, the one who kills the prophets and stones those who are sent to her! How often I wanted to gather your children together, as a hen gathers her chicks under her wings, but you were not willing!"
—MATTHEW 23:37

JOHN CHAPTER 11

Death. Even the word on the page brings feelings of dread and sadness.

John chapter 11 is about death—no wait, it's about life—no, it's *really* about the Lord's perspective on the kind of life that only comes as a result of complete death.

What are we willing to do to see this end? We have to continue to believe when all hope is lost and the people around us have long since given up. We have to know, and I mean *know*, that there is something on the other side of "final."

The death of a career
The death of a marriage
The death of a parent
The death of a child
The death of a dream
The death of hope

I would have lost heart, unless I had believed
that I would see the goodness of the Lord
in the land of the living.
—PSALM 27:13

READ JOHN 11:1–16

The apostle John does not document the "mass healings" that Jesus accomplished during His earthly ministry, but we know from the other gospels that there were several such occasions (Matthew 4:24, 12:15, 15:30, and 19:2; Mark 1:34 and 3:10). John likes to focus on the one: "Now a certain man was sick" (John 11:1).

1. Write everything we know about this man from verses 1 and 2.

2. The Bible does not give us long, flowery descriptions. The Holy Spirit did not choose to pen the words with a "writer's" hand; rather, we see Him use fishermen, shepherds, prophets, physicians, and other tradespeople not necessarily known for expressive speech. Yet, even in its brevity, what does verse 3 tell us about the relationship that Jesus had with this family?

3. Write what the phrase "for the glory of God" means in your own words (verse 4).

4. One of the beautiful things about Jesus walking among us was that He showed us what God was like. If you have ever thought, *God, why is this happening to me?*, you are allowed a glimpse into the mind of God with Jesus's words in verse 4. Incredible. The practical application of this verse for our own lives is limitless. Is there some difficulty in your life right now where this truth can be applied? Share it here.

5. Verse 5 seems to contradict verse 6, but this is Jesus so we know that He did not make a mistake. What might we have expected Jesus to do upon hearing of Lazarus' condition?

6. Write out verse 5 here.

7. This is important because sometimes the Lord does delay. When we don't receive the answer to a prayer within the timeframe we had in mind, what is sometimes our attitude?

8. At this point in the account, we know that Jesus is *aware* of what is happening with his friends and that He *loves* them, but has chosen to stay away from them for two more days. There are no conversations recorded with the disciples until He is ready to move. What are they concerned about (verse 8)?

9. This was obviously a legitimate concern. There was probably an element of fear for their lives as well. Do you think His reply in verses 9 and 10 was meant to comfort them? Write your thoughts.

It appears that they are still trying to talk Him out of going (verse 12) until Jesus's words in verse 14. It cannot be any clearer than that. Jesus was the only one present who knew what He was getting ready to do. He knew that what they were getting ready to witness would solidify, both to His followers and to His enemies, His supremacy over even death.

10. John is the only one to record any words of Thomas. Look at each of these passages and write a few characteristics you see in this man.

John 11:16:

John 14:5:

John 20:26–28:

READ JOHN 11:17–37

It was customary to bury people the day that they died so, at this point, Lazarus had been dead for four days (verse 17). This was not a quiet scene, however. John uses the phrase "many of the Jews" several times in his gospel (11:19, 11:45, 12:9, 12:11, and 19:20). Many commentaries state that John used the phrase to make a distinction between the crowds and those who were the Jewish opposition to Jesus. If that was indeed the case, how wonderful that they were among those present for what was about to take place!

11. Take a look at Mary and Martha in verse 20. What is each doing?

12. Contrast this with Luke 10:38–42. What are your thoughts?

13. We each handle grief differently and for these women, the loss was so real and raw. Each says the same thing to Jesus when she first sees Him (verses 21 and 32). What does this tell you about what they believed of Jesus?

14. Verse 22 is one of my favorites of the entire chapter because even then, four days after her brother's death, Martha had some hope. Have you ever personally felt this kind of hope when all seemed lost?

15. Martha demonstrates that she still believed who Jesus was despite the disappointment of her circumstances (verse 24 and 27). It is not *fact* that will get us there, only *faith*. All of a sudden, her faith was tested. What does she believe (verse 27)?

Doctrinally, Martha had it exactly right. She was completely convinced in her mind who Jesus was, but a death will test us like nothing else. This is the case with physical death, yes, but also the death of a relationship or a ministry or fill in the blank. All of a sudden, she was face to face with what she believed about her Savior.

16. Let's switch to Mary now. There is no conversation recorded between her and Jesus, only her statement to Him in verse 32. Skim verses 28 through 33 and make some observations about Mary. What do you see? What is she doing? How is she behaving?

17. In your opinion, was her behavior honoring to the Lord? Why or why not? (This is not meant to be an argumentative question. I just want us to think through how, as godly women, our emotions might affect our responses to intense situations.)

18. Because we have the benefit of the entire Bible (unlike Mary and Martha), write out a few verses that you personally find comforting in loss.

19. Why do you think "Jesus wept" (verse 35)?

READ JOHN 11:38–44

20. The word *groan* literally means to "snort like a horse" in the Greek.[16] (By the way, it is the same word used in verse 33.) The word choice implies "anger" from our Lord. What was arousing such an emotion for Jesus?

The warning of Martha in verse 39 is so purely practical. By including it, John continues to place us right in the center of the scene and invites us to involve all our senses. I don't know if that would have been my first thought upon hearing Jesus's order to "take away the stone," but it certainly might have been. When the sisters had first involved Jesus in verse 3, they never thought it would go this far. He was *supposed* to heal Lazarus before any of this was even a reality, but yet, there they were.

21. How is "belief" tied to "seeing" (verse 40)?

22. Before the triumph of "Lazarus, come forth" (verse 43), there had to be death. This intense, practical truth jumps off the pages of Scripture for us. How does this speak to you personally?

---

[16] "G1690 - embrimaomai - Strong's Greek Lexicon (nkjv)." Blue Letter Bible. Accessed 29 May, 2023. https://www.blueletterbible.org/lexicon/g1690/nkjv/tr/0-1/

23. It must have been paralyzing for the crowd to see Lazarus walk out of that tomb. The scene that John paints for us in verse 44 is vivid. In the case of Lazarus, grave clothes were the cause for not being free. However, just like Lazarus couldn't live in those grave clothes, we cannot live the lives the Lord has called us to by remaining "bound up" in our pasts. What are some examples of things that will keep believers "out of the tomb" but not completely free?

READ JOHN 11:45–57

24. The reactions to what had just happened were bound to be as varied as they were intense. We are told that "many" believed, which seems to be the most rational choice considering what they had just witnessed. Why do you think that some told the Pharisees (verse 46)?

25. Fear will warp our thinking. The religious leaders demonstrate this reality in verses 47 through 53. They would each have his own responsibilities for what they do with Jesus, but as a group, what was their motivation for seeking to kill Him?

26. We are on the cusp of Jesus's last week before His crucifixion. The disciples barely had time to catch their breath from what they had just witnessed and what was about to change the eternity of every person on this planet. With the information they had at this time, what do you think was their collective attitude?

Oh Death, where is your sting.
—1 Corinthians 15:55

JOHN CHAPTER 12

Chapter 12 begins the countdown, so to speak, to the cross. Everything in Jesus's ministry has led up to this point. The apostle John actually spends seven chapters on events that occurred the week before the crucifixion. That's one-third of his entire book! As a close friend of Jesus, these are the things he remembered many years after they took place. These are the memories that struck such a chord with him that he (inspired by the Holy Spirit) penned them so we might use them to continue to build on the foundation he began in chapter 1.

John knew there was significance to everything Jesus did and that He was the only One who could bring significance to anything we do.

Significance of sacrifice
Significance of surrender
Significance of finally seeing clearly

READ JOHN 12:1–11

1. Most commentators agree that this narrative describes the same event as Matthew 26:6–13 and Mark 14:3–9. However, John includes some details in verses 1 and 2 about who was present that we do not have in the other gospels. Why do you think the apostle John included this group of three when the others accounts fail to mention them by name? (We can only speculate so there is no wrong answer. Of note, John is also the only gospel to record Lazarus's resurrection.)

Jesus had given this family such a gift. I cannot fathom how you return to "real life" after the events of chapter 11. However, the scene John paints for us in verses 1 and 2 could have occurred anytime and anywhere. It's just a meal, but then something else happens.

2. Mary does something that stopped everything. Look at Matthew 26:7, Mark 14:3, and John 12:3 and write every detail mentioned in each.

3. As Judas would later point out (John 12:5), this was a very expensive item. It was probably her dowry or inheritance, but most surely it was the most valuable thing she owned or would ever own. She would never have a replacement. Why do you think she used it in such a way? What could have possibly motivated her to perform such an act?

4. Spikenard is said to have a strong, musky smell. The oil used to anoint Jesus may have been combined with another fragrance to make it even more pleasing to the senses. Even alone, spikenard has a powerful scent and there was a lot of it poured out all at once that day. What are some of the effects of spilling out something very aromatic in a small space?

5. Mary was willing to open herself up to criticism by doing this. We know what Judas was thinking (verses 5–6), but write what some of the other reactions in the room might have been.

6. "But Jesus." Read His response in Matthew 26:10–12, Mark 14:6–8, and John 12:7–8. Why did Jesus allow her to do this?

7. By using the words "day of My burial" (verse 7), Jesus clearly stated what was about to happen. Before He made the agonizing walk to the cross, He would repeat it again and again for them. This was not going to be just another Passover. *His* death brought new significance to *her* sacrifice. What did Jesus mean when He foretold that this act would continue to be told as a "memorial" to her (Matthew 26:13 and Mark 14:9)?

8. Before leaving this section, I want us to think about one more thing. The morning after she anointed Jesus, Mary awoke no longer having her most prized possession. It had been broken and completely spilled out. If there was even an ounce of security for her in that bottle of oil, there could not be any longer. Write any thoughts you have here about this aspect of her sacrifice.

9. What is a practical application you can pull from this account for yourself?

10. There was an understandable curiosity about Lazarus (verse 9), but for the chief priests, the motive was much more sinister. This man's very existence threatened what they held most dear: their power. What do you think they were hoping to gain by killing him?

READ JOHN 12:12–19

Whereas the other gospels go into detail about acquiring the colt (Matthew 21:1–3, Mark 11:1–7, and Luke 19:28–35), the apostle John takes us straight to the show of support for Jesus as He entered Jerusalem. The crowds wanted the oppression from Rome to stop. They wanted their lives to be easier. What they had seen from Jesus over the last few years would appear to accomplish both. That Jesus even allowed such a display was in contrast with all they had seen of Him thus far. It certainly wasn't for lack of opportunity. There had been multiple times that Jesus had a crowd following Him, but the enthusiasm this time could not be bridled and, of course, His time had come.

11. Write out Zechariah 9:9.

Clearly, this was their King. It was happening exactly the way the verse in Zechariah said. Palm branches (verse 13) were a sign of victory and were used by the Romans as well as the Jews as symbols of peace. Matthew 21:8 and Luke 19:36 add that the crowds also threw clothes on the ground before Him.

12. "Hosanna" means "save now" (verse 13) and we know that is exactly what would happen, but it would not be the kind of salvation they were looking for. They wanted a political king and, from what they had seen and heard of Jesus, there was nothing He couldn't do. Why do you think Jesus allowed such a scene to play out as the crowds gathered for Passover?

As the crowds were crying out, "Blessed is He who comes in the name of the Lord," John gives us some insight into what the disciples were thinking (verse 16). They apparently were not thinking of the fulfillment of prophecy unfolding before their eyes. What they did see must have filled them with a kind of hope. Jesus had spoken to them about His death, but what was happening right in front of them was so intense. The crowds appeared to love Him! I would think that they would have replayed this scene over and over again in their minds in the coming weeks.

13. Why did they understand when "Jesus was glorified"? What had changed in them (verse 16)?

14. The raising of Lazarus had done much to spread Jesus's popularity and the Pharisees were obviously aware. From their point of view, at this moment, what was happening (verse 19)?

READ JOHN 12:20–26

15. In his commentary, Warren Wiersbe says that the wording in the original text indicates that these Greeks "were accustomed to come and worship at the feast."[17] These were likely Gentiles who would attend Jewish synagogue. Why do you think they, being non-Jews, would feel comfortable in asking for an audience with Jesus?

16. What did they see in Jesus that made Him approachable?

As Gentiles, they weren't aware of or didn't care about the Pharisees' bias against Jesus. They wouldn't be frightened of the religious leadership of the day. They just wanted to see Him. Actually, the word "see" in verse 21 means "to know." They wanted "to know" Jesus. We really cannot tell from the text if He talked to them or not. We can only speculate on that point, but we do have Jesus's response in verses 24 through 26.

Can you think of a use (a real use) for one (only one) grain of wheat? (I couldn't.) If you only have one grain of wheat, the only shot it has at anything meaningful is to be planted. The seed surrenders its life and then produces much.

17. In applying this truth to our own lives, what does it look like to "hate" your life (verse 25)?

---

[17] Warren W. Wiersbe. *The Bible Exposition Commentary, Volume 1.* (Wheaton: Victor Books, 1989), 341.

18. Why does Jesus require complete surrender (i.e., dying)?

19. After surrender comes service. Why did Jesus connect *following* with *serving* (verse 26)?

READ JOHN 12:27–36

20. Take a look at the following verses. For each reference, write out who is speaking and what He is saying.

Matthew 3:17:

Matthew 17:5:

John 12:28:

21. List some things that all three references have in common.

22. When God the Father spoke, the people who stood by only heard thundering (verse 29). If the people couldn't understand what He said, why do you think Jesus said it was *for* them?

23. How does Jesus "draw all peoples" to Himself with His crucifixion (verse 32)?

Because of the crowd's response in verse 34, many commentators believe that they must have understood that Jesus was referring to His death. They had just hailed Him as their King. No wonder this was confusing for them. Not only did they have to rethink who He was, but they also had to confront what they had been taught about the Messiah from the Old Testament law.

24. What had they been taught? Take a look at each reference and write what it says about the Messiah.

Psalm 72:17:

Psalm 89:36:

Psalm 110:4:

Isaiah 9:7:

Jesus leaves them with words of light and darkness and then "was hidden from them." This appears to mark the end of Jesus's public ministry.

READ JOHN 12:37–50

25. When a person continues in unbelief, what is the danger (verses 39–40)?

26. The Bible does not give us a time frame for this truth. The remedy is found in Isaiah 55:6. What is it?

27. What is the sad commentary of verses 42 and 43?

28. List everything that belief in Jesus will do for us, according to verses 44 through 48.

This chapter began with a woman's sacrificial gift and ended as we moved ever closer to the ultimate sacrifice of our Savior on the cross.

"A light to bring revelation to the Gentiles, and the glory of Your people Israel."
—LUKE 2:32

JOHN CHAPTERS 13 AND 14

Betrayal: To deliver or expose to an enemy by treachery or disloyalty; to be unfaithful in guarding, maintaining, or fulfilling; to disappoint the hopes or expectations of; to reveal or disclose in violation of confidence; to reveal unconsciously (something someone would preferably conceal); to deceive, misguide, or corrupt; to seduce and desert.[18]

We should probably pay more attention to this word because each one of us will experience it, likely more than once. Look how broad the definition is. However, it's an ugly word. It carries with it all kinds of emotion. I can promise you that we will all be caught on both sides of this word in our lifetimes. We will be the betrayed and we will be the betrayer.

Before chapter 13 is finished, Jesus will shine a light on two betrayers. The reaction of each to his betrayal will be significant to how they are remembered by history.

What of Jesus's reaction to the betrayal? That, my friends, is worthy of note because our flesh is so strong in the wake of such an offense. For our Lord, the physical suffering of the cross was coming quickly and the emotional burden of the sin He would carry there was intensifying. Yet, He was betrayed. The Father did not spare Him that.

In hindsight, we know these players—the "bad" guys, if you will—but at the time these events took place, they all looked the same. Everyone sitting around that table looked equal.

---

[18] "Betray." WordReference Random House Learner's Dictionary of American English © 2023. Accessed May 29, 2023. https://www.wordreference.com/definition/betrayal

For the Lord does not see as man sees; for man looks at the
outward appearance, but the Lord looks at the heart.
—1 Samuel 16:7b

READ JOHN 13:1–17

The next five chapters (13 through 17) cover a period of approximately twenty-four hours. John slows things down for us, if you will, so that we don't miss important, personal details of Jesus's final hours before the cross.

1. Who is Jesus's "own" referred to in verse 1?

2. What does the phrase, "He loved them to the end" mean to you (verse 1)?

3. Write out 1 Peter 5:8 here.

4. We know there was no lack in Jesus so, in your opinion, how was the devil able to pull Judas Iscariot's heart away from Him?

5. The act of betrayal rarely comes on suddenly. Usually, things are set into motion over a period of time. Give some examples of the kinds of thoughts and/or feelings that can begin to plant the seeds of betrayal.

6. Look back over verses 1 through 3 and write everything that these verses state that Jesus "knew."

With all these things in His mind, He "took a towel and girded Himself" (verse 4), taking on the appearance of a servant. David Guzik says this about the scene.

> This was more awkward than we might think. First, because of the sandals they wore and the roads they walked on, the feet would be dirty. Second, the disciples would eat a formal meal like this at a table known as a triclinium. This was a low (coffee-table height), U-shaped table. The guests would sit, and their status at the meal was reflected by how close they were seated to the host or leader of the meal. Because the table was low, they didn't sit on chairs. They leaned on pillows, with their feet behind them. This meant that dirty feet could be unpleasantly close to the table during the meal. So, the unwashed feet were conspicuous.[19]

---

[19] Guzik, D. "Study Guide for John 13 by David Guzik." Blue Letter Bible. Last Modified 6/2022. https://www.blueletterbible.org/comm/guzik_david/study-guide/john/john-13.cfm

7. Jesus was the only one who knew of the betrayal at this point, yet His mind was on serving. Even these men who had spent an intense three years with Him appeared to be taken aback by His choice. Why do you think this was so different from anything they had seen from Jesus in the past?

8. John records Peter's reaction specifically in verses 6 through 9. Why do you think John noted Peter's words for us? (Remember that they knew each other before they were called to be disciples.)

9. Could Peter's reaction be a cautionary tale for us? Why or why not?

10. Give a Scripture reference that you believe shows proof that Peter did eventually understand what the Lord was doing that evening (verse 7).

The word translated "wash" in John 13:5–6, 8, 12, and 14 is *nipto*, which means to "wash parts of the body."[20] The word in verse 10 translated "bathed" (NKJV) is *louo*, which is to "wash all over."[21] This distinction is significant because, in verse 10, Jesus begins to broaden their thoughts on what they were observing.

11. If Jesus is speaking of "bathing" as our salvation (as almost every commentator agrees), what is He referring to in using the phrase, "needs only to wash his feet," as the verse continues (verse 10)?

12. Spiritually speaking, how do we "wash our feet"?

13. What are "these things" that Jesus is referring to in verse 17?

READ JOHN 13:18–30

14. Not only had the twelve been with Jesus for three years solid, but they had also been with each other. Why were they "perplexed" (verse 22)?

---

[20] "G3538 - niptō - Strong's Greek Lexicon (nkjv)." Blue Letter Bible. Accessed 29 May, 2023. https://www.blueletterbible.org/lexicon/g3538/nkjv/tr/0-1/
[21] "G3068 - louō - Strong's Greek Lexicon (nkjv)." Blue Letter Bible. Accessed 29 May, 2023. https://www.blueletterbible.org/lexicon/g3068/nkjv/tr/0-1/

In order for the picture in our minds to be correct, we need to make note of how the Jews would eat their meals. They had adopted the Persian custom of reclining on cushions, leaning on the left arm with feet outstretched behind, leaving the right arm free to use while eating. With this information, the positioning mentioned verse 23 makes markedly more sense.

15. In verse 23, the apostle John refers to himself for the first time as the "one whom Jesus loved." What does this tell us about John for him to pen such a description of himself?

For whatever the reason, either closeness of heart or physical proximity, Peter urged John to press Jesus for an answer to the obvious question: "of whom" did He speak regarding the betrayal (verse 24)? Additionally, Matthew, Mark, and Luke broaden our view of what was going on around the entire table (Matt. 26:22, Mark 14:19, and Luke 22:23). All of them wondered, *Is it I?*

16. Take another look at verse 13:2 and then 13:27. What do you think John is implying to us by including both verses, somewhat like bookends?

17. John's account does much more for us than simply hit the highlights. Verses 27 through 29 illustrate the intimacy of the setting and closeness of the participants. Judas was a guy they all knew. I don't think we can make the mistake of thinking that Judas wore his betrayal on his face. Write your thoughts here.

READ JOHN 13:31–35

18. Upon the exit of Judas, there is a change in how Jesus addresses those remaining of the group. What does He call them in verse 33?

19. This must have made an impression on John, as he uses the same phrase nine times in 1 John. What does this term of endearment imply in a relationship?

20. How would the world know they were His disciples (verse 35)?

21. Certainly the same is true for us. Why does this set us apart even today?

READ JOHN 13:36–38

This short discourse between Peter and Jesus held much heartache for both. Read the verses out loud. Read them once more. Read them one more time.

22. Now, write your thoughts.

I, the Lord, search the heart; I test the mind.
—Jeremiah 17:10a

READ JOHN 14:1–6

23. Make a list of everything (or as many as you have room for) troubling you in your life right now.

24. Now, what does verse 1 say is the cure for a troubled heart?

25. How is "belief" the answer?

26. The word *prepare* in verse 2 means "to make ready."[22] What are some of the motivations in preparing something for someone?

---

22 "G2090 - hetoimazō - Strong's Greek Lexicon (nkjv)." Blue Letter Bible. Accessed 29 May, 2023. https://www.blueletterbible.org/lexicon/g2090/nkjv/tr/0-1/

27. Thomas asks a question that was probably on the minds of more than one around the table that evening (verse 5): "Where exactly was He going?" If they were going to be with Him, as He said, they should know where that was. In His reply, Jesus makes it abundantly clear that He was going to be with the Father and the only way to get there was through Him. When Jesus gives us access to the Father, what are some of the benefits of that relationship for us?

READ JOHN 14:7–11

28. Philip wants to see God. We all want to see God. In our pain, in our confusion, in our search for answers, we want to see God. What does Jesus tell Philip (and us) about Himself and the Father in this section of Scripture?

29. Believing this is essential to our faith. Why?

READ JOHN 14:12–14

30. What does the phrase, "Whatever you ask 'in My name'" mean to you? How do we know something is "in His name"?

READ JOHN 14:15–18

31. Write everything we can learn about the Holy Spirit from these verses.

READ JOHN 14:19–24

32. Verse 21 begins with the same truth as verse 15. What "commandments" is Jesus talking about in these verses?

33. How does my love for Him motivate me to do what He says?

34. Ultimately, if a person does not love Jesus, he or she will not "keep" His words, but that person will have chosen poorly. What is a nonbeliever choosing if he or she does not choose Jesus?

READ JOHN 14:25–31

35. How is the peace that Jesus gives different from that of the world (verse 27)?

36. Jesus was not distracted by the betrayal that was to come. He had many things to tell the disciples before leaving them for the cross. Think back over the truths Jesus touched on in chapters 13 and 14 and write one that was particularly sweet to you personally.

"Let not your heart be troubled, neither let it be afraid."
—John 14:27c

JOHN CHAPTERS 15 AND 16

"These things I have spoken:"

- that you will have joy (John 15:11);
- that you will be steady (John 16:1); and
- that you will know peace (John 16:33).

If the words of Jesus are going to make any practical difference in my life at all, there are certain things that need to happen. I need to hear them. I need to understand them. I need to believe them.

Hearing His words is really not that difficult in America. Now, I realize there are probably people in our country who have never heard of Jesus, but certainly a vast majority of American homes have a Bible (or many Bibles) and are located within a reasonable travel distance of some kind of church.

Understanding His words can also be accessed because of the resources so readily available at our fingertips day or night. There is no end to the amount of commentary that has been written on the Word of God.

Believing. Therein lies the real key and the real challenge because it begins on the inside and it is so very personal. It starts in that place that is so deep no one else has ever seen it. Not only is it deep, it also has a tendency to jump and move and veer. One minute, my faith is so solid, it seems that nothing will budge it. The next minute, I cannot begin to remember what a firm foundation even looks like.

As Jesus speaks to the eleven left in the room in chapters 15 and 16, there are things that made sense at the time, but would mean more later. There are things that made *no* sense whatsoever at the time, but would become clearer later. There were things that would have made them sad and discouraged to hear, but upon recollection, would turn everything they had heard from Him previously into a future and a hope.

READ JOHN 15:1–8

1. Why do you think Jesus chose to illustrate His point with the word picture of a grapevine?

2. In verse 2, we are dealing with two different kinds of branches. What are they?

Based on the words "in Me" in verse 2, J. Vernon McGee teaches that this section of Scripture (verses 1–8) deals with fruit bearing, not salvation.[23] We will also look at the verses from this perspective. This is important to note, as it will change how we read verse 2.

3. In each case, the branch is getting attention from the vinedresser: the unfruitful is taken away, and the fruitful is pruned. If the verse is talking about the unfruitful Christian life versus the fruitful Christian life, what could it look like to be "taken away" by the vinedresser?

---

[23] McGee, J. "Comments for John by Dr. J. Vernon McGee." Blue Letter Bible. Last Modified 15 Nov 2017. https://www.blueletterbible.org/Comm/mcgee_j_vernon/notes-outlines/john/john-comments.cfm

4. Do some research on your own on pruning. What did you discover about this task?

5. Write a definition of *abide*.

6. What does it look like to "abide" in Jesus (verse 4)?

7. What are some examples of "fruit" that come as a result of abiding (verse 5)?

8. Jesus spoke these things to give us joy, keep us steady, and bring us peace. How do verses 1 through 8

bring you joy?

keep you steady?

give you peace?

READ JOHN 15:9–17

9. As the disciples heard Jesus say, "keep My commandments," I wonder if their minds were spinning. They had been with Him three years by that point, but He made it simple for them. Write the commandment He gave them in verse 12.

10. When Jesus says, "as I have loved you," think back over the previous chapters in John and list some examples of how He had loved them.

11. What did He use to distinguish between servants and friends (verse 15)?

12. How does the expectation change between a servant and a friend?

13. Jesus spoke these things to give us joy, keep us steady, and bring us peace. How do verses 9 through 17

bring you joy?

keep you steady?

give you peace?

READ JOHN 15:18–16:4

14. From verses 18 through 25, list all the reasons the world will hate us.

15. Sometimes, we are shocked by the world's behavior towards us. What are some benefits for a believer in remembering the truth of verse 19?

16. The disciples had to have known that their own persecution could be coming. The Pharisees were becoming progressively more hostile toward Jesus throughout His public ministry. If we are forewarned of impending persecution, what are some practical ways we can prepare for it?

17. Jesus spoke these things to give us joy, keep us steady, and bring us peace. How do verses 15:18–16:4

bring you joy?

keep you steady?

give you peace?

READ JOHN 16:5–15

18. Why was it to their benefit that Jesus was going away (verse 7)?

19. Even though His leaving was to their advantage, He realized it was hard for them to hear. Have you ever heard something you believed was from the Lord that was very difficult? Write it here.

20. In this section of Scripture, Jesus details for us how the Holy Spirit operates. Read back over verses 5 through 15 and make a list of the work of the Holy Spirit

In the world

In the disciples

21. The above list is still true. The Holy Spirit works in the world and in believers the same way. However, many denominations and churches largely ignore or do not acknowledge His work. Why is it important that the Holy Spirit, and His work in our lives, is taught today?

22. Jesus spoke these things to give us joy, keep us steady, and bring us peace. How do verses 16:5–15

bring you joy?

keep you steady?

give you peace?

READ JOHN 16:16–33

If we forget that the Lord's disciples were just ordinary men, we will lose the intensity and barrage of emotion that filled the room that night. There was confusion, yes, but they had been confused before. There was sadness, but, again, they had been sad before. Over the previous three years while they were in the presence of Jesus, they experienced things, many of which would only make sense long after His ascension. As this private time with them was winding down that night, He focused on joy and hope.

23. In breaking down verse 20, how do you think the phrase "but the world will rejoice" made them feel?

It is heartbreaking to think that people would be happy when your friend, your leader, your rabbi was killed. Indeed, we do have their reaction documented for us in Matthew 27 and Mark 15. In the midst of the sorrow, Jesus assured them that there would be joy coming for them.

24. Verse 22 describes a joy that "no one will take from you." What makes this kind of joy so special?

25. In verses 23 through 28, Jesus focuses on prayer. He indicates that there was going to be a change in their praying. From these verses, what do you see that was going to be different for them?

26. How do we know we are asking something "in His name" (verses 23–24)?

27. What are some things that will give us peace in the world?

28. How is the peace that Jesus gives different from that of the world (verse 33)?

29. Jesus spoke these things to give us joy, keep us steady, and bring us peace. How do verses 16:16–33

bring you joy?

keep you steady?

give you peace?

He who is in you is greater than he who is in the world.
—1 JOHN 4:4B

JOHN CHAPTERS 17 AND 18

Therefore, know that the Lord your God, He is God, the faithful
God who keeps covenant and mercy for a thousand generations
with those who love Him and keep His commandments.
—DEUTERONOMY 7:9

There is none more faithful than our God. As believers, we base our eternities on the fact that God has always *been* faithful and will always *be* faithful. As He moved closer to the cross, Jesus remained faithful—faithful to His Father, faithful to His disciples and faithful to His purpose. We are called to be like Jesus. We are called to be faithful.

It must not be an impossible task, this "being faithful," because in Psalm 31:23, we read, "the Lord preserves the *faithful*." and Psalm 101:6a says, "My eyes shall be on the *faithful* of the land." There must be a way to fulfill this calling.

How's your prayer life?

To the praying soul there becomes possible and natural the obedience
which is the daily walk of the disciple with the unseen God.[24]
—R. A. TORREY

It is a privilege to hear the prayer of someone who has walked closely with the Lord for many years. The tone of that prayer will reveal a familiarity that is the natural byproduct of many hours spent pouring out his or her heart before a God that he or she is certain

---

[24] Torrey, R. "Divine Efficacy of Prayer by R. A. Torrey." Blue Letter Bible. Last Modified 6 Oct, 2003. https://www.blueletterbible.org/Comm/torrey_ra/fundamentals/79.cfm

has heard. Think of it: being absolutely certain that the God of the universe has heard something that you said, and believing Him to be faithful.

In chapter 17, we are allowed to listen in as Jesus spends some of His precious time before the cross in prayer. Even then, Jesus is praying for believers (Romans 8:34 and Hebrews 7:25) at the right hand of the Father.

READ JOHN 17

1. In verse 1, Jesus says, "The hour has come." We have seen four other places in the book of John where Jesus states His hour had *not* yet come. Find all four and write the references here.

2. Every part of Jesus's earthly ministry had led up to this point. "The hour has come." How will the Son be glorified?

3. The word *glorify* in verse 1 means "to do honor to, to make glorious."[25] How will the Son glorify the Father?

---

[25] "G1392 - doxazō - Strong's Greek Lexicon (nkjv)." Blue Letter Bible. Accessed 30 May, 2023. https://www.blueletterbible.org/lexicon/g1392/nkjv/tr/0-1/

4. Jesus says, "that they may know You" (verse 3). Practically, what does "knowing God" look like?

5. Jesus prays specifically for His disciples in verses 6 through 19. The disciples had been good students (with the exception of Judas Iscariot). Make a list here of things that Jesus specifically mentions in His prayer for them that they have done well.

6. Now make a list of specific things Jesus is praying for them in verses 6 through 19.

7. Jesus knew these eleven and He also knew what He was leaving them to do in the years that followed. They would desperately need the list you have put together in question 6 above. Certainly, one of the reasons He prayed was that this group was going to be "sent into the world." How can they be "in the world" and not "of the world" (verse 16)?

8. What a blessing that we, too, are included in Jesus's prayer that evening. Verses 20 through 26 are about *all* believers—"those who will believe." The church was about to be born because of the word of these disciples. The importance of their mission is clearly stated by our Lord. In your opinion, what is one thing that verse 20 says about the mindset of Jesus prior to going to the cross?

9. Jesus prays for the unity of all believers in verse 21. How do we reconcile our different denominations and worship styles with having unity among all believers?

10. Verse 21 says, "that the world may *believe*" and verse 23 includes the phrase, "that the world may *know*." Why do you think Jesus made this distinction? What is the difference between the two?

11. Jesus closes out this prayer in verses 25 and 26 in victory. There is no indication of the sorrow that was coming, but only the declaration of triumph that resulted from that sorrow. In reading back over His prayer, we can see what was most important to Jesus at this hour. What stands out to you personally in chapter 17?

READ JOHN 18:1–11

"When Jesus had spoken these words, He went out." Matthew Henry writes "That having by His sermon prepared His disciples for this hour of trial, and by His prayer prepared Himself for it, He then courageously went out to meet it."[26] His hour had come.

Because of the Passover lambs being sacrificed, the Brook Kidron would have run red with blood when Jesus and His eleven crossed it before coming to the Garden of Gethsemane. The commentaries state that this was a private garden, belonging to a friend of Jesus, who had given Him a key so He would be granted free access whenever He chose. It was a place they went often (verse 2).

12. What does it indicate to us about Jesus that He went to such a familiar spot?

13. Judas knew Jesus and His disciples. In fact, he knew them all very well, having spent the last three years with the group. Why do you think he came with such a strong presence to the garden that night (verse 3)?

Nothing that was happening came as a surprise to Jesus (verse 4) and He proved that He was in complete control of the situation by approaching His would-be captors with a question. While His demeanor may not have surprised Judas, the group with him may have been taken aback. I wonder if they had ever encountered a fugitive so willing to be taken. The word He is in italics in your Bible because it was added later in verses 5 and 6. What Jesus actually said was, "I am." Look at Exodus 3:13–14. Simply amazing.

---

[26] Henry, M. "Commentary on John 18 by Matthew Henry." Blue Letter Bible. Last Modified 1 Mar, 1996. https://www.blueletterbible.org/Comm/mhc/Jhn/Jhn_018.cfm

14. What caused their fall to the ground (verse 6)?

15. If they fell to the ground, it stands to reason that they had to get back up in order to finish arresting Him—and they were carrying lanterns and torches. These details are important in picturing the scene of confusion that must have been unfolding. John is the only one to record these particulars. There probably was little time to think. Everyone was just reacting—everyone, that is, except Jesus. What does He tell the detachment of troops in verse 8?

16. Each of the gospels tells of Peter's use of the sword in verse 10 (although none of the other gospels mentions his name). Why do you think Peter was swinging the sword?

17. Luke, the physician, is the only one to record what happened to the injured man. Look at Luke 22:51 and write what Jesus did.

18. Jesus didn't tell Peter to get rid of his sword, just to put it away (verse 11). We know the reason he has the sword. Look at Luke 22:35–38. Does that piece of information change your answer to question 16? Why or why not?

READ JOHN 18:12–14

19. Why do you think they bound Him (verse 12)?

20. Annas had been high priest until being removed by the Romans for corruption. His son-in-law, Caiaphas, was now the high priest. Warren Wiersbe states in his commentary that the high priest's family was generally believed to be in charge of temple business.[27] Can you think of any reason why this "ruling" family might have been unhappy with Jesus?

READ JOHN 18:15–18

Most commentators agree that the unnamed disciple mentioned in verse 15 was John himself. There could have been some family connection that made him "known to the high priest" (verse 16). If true, it would actually explain two details in this narrative that might otherwise be hard to get past. The first was that he was allowed to return for Peter to bring him in. The second was why he was not asked the same questions that Peter was regarding his connection to Jesus.

---

[27] Warren W. Wiersbe. *The Bible Exposition Commentary, Volume 1*. (Wheaton: Victor Books, 1989), 375.

21. Peter denied Jesus first to a servant girl. She was a young girl and held no authority whatsoever. Yet Peter denied his friend, his rabbi, his Savior (John 6:68–69) in answer to her simple question. Sometimes we will surprise ourselves how quickly we deny Him. What do you think are some reasons for Peter's denial? (They are probably the same as our own.)

22. We know that someone (possibly John) had brought Peter into the courtyard, but now they appear to be separated. Where is Peter in verse 18?

23. What is a practical lesson that can be taken from this picture?

READ JOHN 18:19–27

24. In verse 21, Jesus basically calls out a matter of law. According to Jewish rule, witnesses were heard first. The high priest appears to be asking Him to incriminate Himself. Another breach of law was that this trial was being held at night (the timeline becomes clearer in John 18:28). List some reasons that the law appears to have become of little consequence when it came to Jesus.

25. There is a strong church tradition that Mark wrote his gospel from accounts that were personally told to him by Peter. With this in mind, read Mark 14:69–72 regarding Peter's second and third denials. Write some details from this passage that are not mentioned in John.

READ JOHN 18:28–40

The religious rulers of Israel could not carry out a death sentence. For that, they needed Roman intervention. Enter Pilate. Pontius Pilate was a Roman governor under the emperor Tiberius. He had sole authority in matters of execution. The part he played in the trial of Jesus would be the thing for which he is most remembered.

Each of the gospels mentions Jesus's time in Pilate's court, but no other gives us a record of the conversation between the two. It is incredible to think as we read John 18:33–38 that Pilate has no idea that he is having a dialogue with the living God Himself. Jesus allowed Himself to be put on trial by His creation, "and we beheld His glory" (John 1:14b).

26. Read through this conversation between Jesus and Pilate and make note of what attributes you see being made manifest in Jesus.

27. Write a definition of "mob mentality."

28. What had happened to this "mob" between John 12:12 and John 18:40?

The cross is drawing near.

Yet it pleased the Lord to bruise Him.
—ISAIAH 53:10

JOHN CHAPTER 19

In writing his gospel, John appears to have made it a goal to record events and details that the other gospel writers had omitted. As mentioned previously, this is one of the things that makes John's account unique.

While Matthew, Mark, and Luke all mention Pilate, John actually records the verbal exchange between him and Jesus in John 18:33–38. He includes certain details of Pilate's indecision in determining a course of action regarding Jesus in chapter 19, verses 5 through 16.

The soldiers, His mother Mary, Nicodemus, and the words "it is finished" are all snapshots of the day of the crucifixion. They come alive for us because of the "one whom Jesus loved." Chapter 19 was penned by a man who wanted to document some of the specifics of a day that would define eternity for humankind.

READ JOHN 19:1–16

1. Chapter 19 appears to jump in mid-scene. As we closed out chapter 18, the crowds (mobs, really) were crying out for Barabbas to be released. It would have been loud and crowded with so many people. With this backdrop, what do you think Pilate was hoping for regarding Jesus at this point (John 18:28–38)?

2. In spite of these things, Pilate took Him to be scourged (v.1). Why?

According to the *Expositor's Greek Testament*, the following describes scourging.

> The victim of this severe punishment was bound in a stooping attitude to a low column and beaten with rods or scourged with whips, the thongs of which were weighted with lead, and studded with sharp-pointed pieces of bone, so that frightful laceration followed each stroke. Death frequently resulted.[28]

After the beating, Jesus is paraded once again before the crowd along with Pilate's second pronouncement that he finds "no fault in Him" (v. 4). Some commentators suggest that Pilate was attempting to gain sympathy for Jesus with such a display. Whatever his motivation, the crowd was unwilling to change their plea. "Crucify Him! Crucify Him!"

3. Write 2 Corinthians 5:21.

4. The NLT version of this verse reads, "that we could be made right with God through Christ." This is what it would take for you and me to be made right with God. Why did it have to be so brutal?

---

[28] "Expositor's Greek Testament." John 19:1. Bible Hub. Accessed May 30, 2023. https://biblehub.com/commentaries/john/19-1.htm

5. "Yet it pleased the LORD to bruise Him" (Isaiah 53:10). The fulfillment of this verse is exactly what the crowds were seeing right before their eyes that day. How do we reconcile a loving God and the cruel scene that is being played out in chapter 19?

6. In verse 8, Pilate heard something that made him "more afraid." What did he hear that made him react in such a way?

7. Pilate appears to be aware that there was something different about this man standing in front of him. He was obviously not an ordinary prisoner. Skim back over 19:1–16 along with 18:28–38 and list some specific indicators that Pilate had pause to convict Jesus. (For added clarity, you may also reference Matthew, Mark, and Luke.)

8. Most commentators agree that Jesus is referring to Caiaphas or, at the very least, the Sanhedrin in verse 11b. Why would they have the "greater sin"?

9. What do you make of the fact that it is the religious leaders who said, "We have no king but Caesar!" (verse 15)?

READ JOHN 19:17–24

For those of us who know Jesus as our Savior, the cross is a symbol of victory. To Pilate and everyone living in Jerusalem in that day, the cross was an emblem of shame. In fact, the Roman statesman-philosopher Cicero said this of crucifixion: "It was the most cruel and shameful of all punishments. Let it never come near the body of a Roman citizen; nay, not even near his thoughts or eyes or ears."[29] *Jesus* is the difference.

10. Explain in your own words why the cross is beautiful to the saved and redeemed.

11. In his commentary, Warren Wiersbe tells us that it was required that the "criminal wear a placard announcing his crime."[30] This would explain verse 19. This was indeed the charge against Jesus. Why do you think it was written in three languages? List a practical reason and a spiritual reason.

Practical:

Spiritual:

12. It was standard procedure for the soldiers at a crucifixion to divide the belongings of the condemned. In the case of Jesus, the soldiers were fulfilling prophecy in doing so. It is a great reminder to us that the Lord will use whomever and whatever He wishes to accomplish His purpose. Why is it important to us that John (or the other writers of the gospels) point out when prophecy was fulfilled that day?

---

[29] Guzik, D. "Study Guide for John 19 by David Guzik." Blue Letter Bible. Last Modified 6/2022. https://www. blueletterbible.org/comm/guzik_david/study-guide/john/john-19.cfm

[30] Warren W. Wiersbe. *The Bible Exposition Commentary, Volume 1.* (Wheaton: Victor Books, 1989), 382.

READ JOHN 19:25–27

13. In a practical sense, what do you think verses 26 and 27 meant for Mary and for John?

READ JOHN 19:28-37.

14. What is Jesus referring to with the words "It is finished." in verse 30?

15. Why is the phrase "He gave up His spirit" so important to this verse?

It was a "high day" because that year the Passover feast commenced on the Sabbath. The Jews had a predicament. It was customary in those days for the Romans to leave the body of the executed person hanging on the cross until it had been devoured by birds or animals. A horrific picture, to be sure, and thus the reason for their plea to Pilate recorded in verse 31.

16. We have an eyewitness account in front of us. What is the reason John gives for writing these things down (verse 35)?

17. What does he want us to "believe"?

READ JOHN 19:38–42

18. Write all the information that can be gained about the man who asked for Jesus's body from these verses: Matthew 27:57, Mark 15:43, Luke 23:50–51, and John 19:38.

19. Read John 3:1–21 and 7:45–52 again. Write your thoughts about the man Nicodemus and where he finds himself in verse 39.

20. Some commentators are critical of these men because of their apparent fear of having their names surrounded with words such as "fear," "secretly," and "by night." However, the opinions of the commentators are simply that: opinions. What are your personal thoughts about these men?

"Just as the Son of Man did not come to be served, but to serve, and to give His life a ransom for many."
—MATTHEW 20:28

As chapter 19 closes, there is darkness and despair, but Sunday's coming.

JOHN CHAPTER 20

The empty tomb is of no comfort if certain questions are not answered. Where was the body of Jesus and by what means did His body leave this place? When faced with difficulty, emotion can cloud our reasoning and cause us to draw out false conclusions. The danger in that, of course, would be that we miss what the Lord has already done right in front of our eyes.

You see, the empty tomb changes *everything*. While the cross means our sins are dealt with, the empty tomb means hope—forever and eternal hope. From that day on, within every situation that the believer finds himself or herself in, there can be hope when viewed through the lens of the empty tomb. If our Savior could beat death so soundly, what can He do for us!

"He is not here; for He is risen, as He said."
MATTHEW 28:6A

****

READ JOHN 20:1–10

1. Take a look at Matthew 28:1, Mark 16:1, and Luke 24:1. List the names of the women who went to the tomb that morning and their purposes.

2. What are your thoughts on the fact that women were the first there?

3. In Mark's gospel, we learn that the group was concerned about moving the stone. This was a very practical thing to be wondering about. They could not have moved it on their own. It would have been impossible. However, it turns out that they needn't have given it a thought. Write out the practical lesson every one of us should pull from this simple truth.

4. The commentators almost all agree that John mentions only Mary Magdalene in his gospel to account for how Peter and he found out about the empty tomb. Why do you suppose she chose to seek these two out in particular? (This exercise is not meant to impose anything onto the text where it is otherwise silent. It is simply to continue to focus our minds on the fact that these were *real* people caught up in *real* situations.)

5. Our text in John's gospel prior to chapter 20 left him at the foot of the cross with Mary (John 19:25–27) and Peter, who had denied even knowing Jesus a few nights earlier (John 18:25–27). Now they are both together running toward the tomb. What do you think was the initial motivation of each?

6. The word *saw* appears in verses 5, 6, and 8, but in the Greek, there are actually three separate words being used, each with its own distinct meaning. In verse 5, the Greek word is *blepo* and it means "to see something, to look at."[31] In verse 6, the Greek word is *theoreo*, meaning "to study, to view attentively."[32] Lastly, in verse 8, the Greek word is *eido* which means "to perceive the significance of."[33] If we only look at the English, we can definitely miss some things from the original text. Reread verses 5 through 8 and write something that you noticed upon being aware of the Greek words discussed in those verses that you may have missed the first time through.

7. Why do you think they went back "to their own homes" (verse 10)?

READ JOHN 20:11–18

8. Mary was just so sad. There are, of course, times when sadness and tears are the only appropriate responses. We serve a God who does not condemn our tears. Write at least two Scripture references that will encourage us in the midst of great sadness.

---

[31] "G991 - blepō - Strong's Greek Lexicon (kjv)." Blue Letter Bible. Accessed 30 May, 2023. https://www.blueletterbible.org/lexicon/g991/kjv/tr/0-1/

[32] "G2334 - theōreō - Strong's Greek Lexicon (kjv)." Blue Letter Bible. Accessed 30 May, 2023. https://www.blueletterbible.org/lexicon/g2334/kjv/tr/0-1/

[33] "G1492 - eidō - Strong's Greek Lexicon (kjv)." Blue Letter Bible. Accessed 30 May, 2023. https://www.blueletterbible.org/lexicon/g1492/kjv/tr/0-1/

9. What is her apparent reaction to the angels she sees right in front of her (verse 12)?

10. Why do you think she does not recognize Jesus (verse 14)?

11. What does Jesus do that leads Mary to realize who He is (verse 16)?

12. Her inclination to fall at His feet and worship would certainly be understandable. Why do you think He forbade that act at this time (verse 17)?

READ JOHN 20:19–23

13. A lot happened "the same day." The word was spreading about His resurrection. Why would they still be afraid of the Jews (verse 19)?

14. The words "Peace be still" had been said by Jesus to the group on other occasions. Do you think the phrase had a different significance this time to them (verse 19)?

15. When Jesus says, "*Receive* the Holy Spirit," that would imply that it is a choice. In other words, He [the Holy Spirit] could be received or rejected. Think back to previous chapters in John when Jesus talked about the Holy Spirit. List some practical ways the Holy Spirit was equipping them to be "sent" (verse 21).

16. Who is the only one who has the power to forgive sins? Use Scripture to back up your answer.

17. If that is the case, what do you think Jesus means in verse 23?

READ JOHN 20:24–29

18. There have been many conclusions drawn regarding Thomas over the many years since John penned his gospel. Looking over these six verses as a whole, jot down a few positives and a few negatives that you see regarding Thomas and his "conditional" belief.

Positives

Negatives

19. What are some things that this section shows us about Jesus?

READ JOHN 20:30–31

20. Write out the following verses.

John 19:35:

John 20:31:

1 John 5:13:

21. What is the common thread?

22. How is being aware of an author's purpose in writing of benefit to the reader?

And these things we write to you that your joy may be full.
—1 John 1:4

JOHN CHAPTER 21

Personally, I do not know what it feels like to fish all night long and catch nothing. The tedium of sitting in a boat with a net in the water and not so much as a nibble to at least spur me on to sit there for another hour sounds tortuous. Uggg.

I do, however, have some idea what it is like to work at something for an extended period of time to no avail, to strive toward a goal that is yielding no positive results, or to continue to push because it is something I'm *supposed* to be able to do. Uggg.

What happened to bring me to this place of frustration? What caused me to throw my net in the water in the first place?

We all have different thresholds for waiting. Obviously, our ages play a factor along with our levels of material comfort while we wait. At some point, we want to *do* something, anything really—we just want motion of some kind.

Jesus was alive. They knew that. However, the question of "what happens next" had yet to be answered for His closest group of followers—so, they fished. They were fisherman, after all, and if things didn't make sense, they could always fish. Right?

READ JOHN 21:1–14

1. Whether going back to fish was a good idea or not depends on the motivation behind it. Since we have no way of knowing their motivations with certainty, we can only speculate. In your opinion, was it a positive or a negative that they threw their nets back in the water that day?

2. We need to be careful not to base our opinions for the first question on the results of their efforts. Just because they "caught nothing" (verse 3) would not necessarily mean it was a bad idea that they were fishing. List some reasons they may have had empty nets that day.

3. Why do you think Jesus asked them the question in verse 5?

4. It is fascinating to me that they actually did what the "stranger" instructed in verse 6. Obviously, if they had known it was Jesus, they would have obeyed immediately based on what they knew to be true of Him. However, the text indicates that they did not know it was Him at that point (verse 4). Picture them pulling the net up from the left side and placing it down into the water on the right side of the boat. These are experienced fishermen. Why were they listening to the man on the shore?

5. Verse 7 is one of my favorites in the entire Bible. John's reaction is priceless! Once he puts everything together that it is Jesus on the shoreline, he exclaims, "It is the Lord!" Have you had a time in your life when you suddenly realized that the Lord was the One orchestrating your circumstances? Write about it here.

6. John remembered and recorded the number of fish for us—so great a drought (nothing) to so great an abundance (153). They knew it was nothing that they had done themselves. Yet, Jesus tells them, "Bring some of the fish you have just caught" (v. 10). Does this tell you anything personally about the heart of our God?

READ JOHN 21:15–19

7. In my Bible, the heading over this section is "Jesus Restores Peter." Although the headings are not considered "inspired" Scripture, they can help us determine the direction of the text. Why might Peter feel the need to be "restored"?

8. When we fail, we can fall into the trap of believing all kinds of lies. Give some examples of what the enemy tries to tell us after we have sinned against the Lord.

9. What are some practical reasons Jesus may have asked Peter the same question three times when He already knows everything about us (verses 15, 16, and 17)?

10. After Peter responds, write Jesus's instruction in each verse.

Verse 15:

Verse 16:

Verse 17:

11. The questions and responses of Jesus dealt with Peter's *love*. Maybe this was the heart of the issue for Peter. Maybe this was what he needed to hear and evaluate. "Peter, do you love Me?" Maybe what Peter *thought* he was doing to show that he loved Jesus was not what the Lord had really asked him to do at all. What are a few practical ways that Peter would indeed take care of Jesus's sheep? Use Scripture to back up your answers.

READ JOHN 21:20–25

12. What is the practical lesson of verses 21 through 22 straight from the mouth of Jesus Himself for all of us?

13. The enemy will try to use the comparison trap on us all the time. It's one of his favorites. Why is this tactic so effective with believers?

14. As we come to the end of the book of John, the apostle seems to want to set the record straight about something. From verse 23, what is he clearing up for all time and eternity?

15. Why do you think it was important to John to address this particular point?

16. "Many other things." Many other teachings, many other miracles, many other kindnesses—the scope of Jesus's earthly ministry could never be fully recorded. How can this truth be of practical help to the believer today?

★★★★★★★★

17. Before we completely leave the book of John, write a personal truth that you gained from your study of this book for yourself.

The grass withers and the flower fades, but
the Word of our God stands forever.
—Isaiah 40:8

BIBLIOGRAPHY

Butler, Trent C. *Holman Bible Dictionary*. Nashville, TN: Holman Bible Publishers, 1991.

Halley, Henry H. *Halley's Bible Handbook*. Grand Rapids, MI: Zondervan, 1996.

Wiersbe, Warren W. *The Bible Exposition Commentary, Volume 1*. Wheaton, IL: Victor Books, 1989.

"They Left Their Nets Behind," That the World May Know, accessed April 18, 2023, https://www.thattheworldmayknow.com/they-left-their-nets-behind.

"John 1 (KJV) - And the Word was made." Blue Letter Bible. Accessed 25 May, 2023. https://www.blueletterbible.org/kjv/jhn/1/14/s_998014

Guzik, David. "Study Guide for Deuteronomy 18 by David Guzik." Blue Letter Bible. Last Modified 6/2022. https://www.blueletterbible.org/comm/guzik_david/study-guide/deuteronomy/deuteronomy-18.cfm

"G755 - architriklinos - Strong's Greek Lexicon (nkjv)." Blue Letter Bible. Accessed 25 May, 2023. https://www.blueletterbible.org/lexicon/g755/nkjv/tr/0-1/

"Expositor's Greek Testament." John 2:14. Bible Hub. Accessed May 25, 2023. https://biblehub.com/commentaries/egt/john/2.htm

Vine, W. E. "Disciple - Vine's Expository Dictionary of New Testament Words." Blue Letter Bible. Last Modified 24 Jun, 1996. https://www.blueletterbible.org/search/Dictionary/viewTopic.cfm

Guzik, David. "Study Guide for John 4 by David Guzik." Blue Letter Bible. Last Modified 6/2022. https://www.blueletterbible.org/comm/guzik_david/study-guide/john/john-4.cfm

"Sea of Galilee," Britannica, accessed April 18, 2023, https://www.britannica.com/place/Sea-of-Galilee.

"G1111 - gongyzō - Strong's Greek Lexicon (nkjv)." Blue Letter Bible. Accessed 29 May, 2023. https://www.blueletterbible.org/lexicon/g1111/nkjv/tr/0-1/

"G2296 - thaumazō - Strong's Greek Lexicon (nkjv)." Blue Letter Bible. Accessed 29 May, 2023. https://www.blueletterbible.org/lexicon/g2296/nkjv/tr/0-1/

Guzik, David. "Study Guide for John 7 by David Guzik." Blue Letter Bible. Last Modified 6/2022. https://www.blueletterbible.org/comm/guzik_david/study-guide/john/john-7.cfm

"G4100 - pisteuō - Strong's Greek Lexicon (kjv)." Blue Letter Bible. Accessed 29 May, 2023. https://www.blueletterbible.org/lexicon/g4100/kjv/tr/0-1/

Schoenian, Susan. "Basic Sheep Info." Sheep101.info. Last modified 4/2021. Accessed May 29, 2023. http://www.sheep101.info/bahavior.html

"G1690 - embrimaomai - Strong's Greek Lexicon (nkjv)." Blue Letter Bible. Accessed 29 May, 2023. https://www.blueletterbible.org/lexicon/g1690/nkjv/tr/0-1/

"Betray." WordReference Random House Learner's Dictionary of American English © 2023. Accessed May 29, 2023. https://www.wordreference.com/definition/betrayal

Guzik, David. "Study Guide for John 13 by David Guzik." Blue Letter Bible. Last Modified 6/2022. https://www.blueletterbible.org/comm/guzik_david/study-guide/john/john-13.cfm

"G3538 - niptō - Strong's Greek Lexicon (nkjv)." Blue Letter Bible. Accessed 29 May, 2023. https://www.blueletterbible.org/lexicon/g3538/nkjv/tr/0-1/

"G3068 - louō - Strong's Greek Lexicon (nkjv)." Blue Letter Bible. Accessed 29 May, 2023. https://www.blueletterbible.org/lexicon/g3068/nkjv/tr/0-1/

"G2090 - hetoimazō - Strong's Greek Lexicon (nkjv)." Blue Letter Bible. Accessed 29 May, 2023. https://www.blueletterbible.org/lexicon/g2090/nkjv/tr/0-1/

McGee, J. Vernon. "Comments for John by Dr. J. Vernon McGee." Blue Letter Bible. Last Modified 15 Nov 2017. https://www.blueletterbible.org/Comm/mcgee_j_vernon/notes-outlines/john/john-comments.cfm

Torrey, R. A. "Divine Efficacy of Prayer by R. A. Torrey." Blue Letter Bible. Last Modified 6 Oct, 2003. https://www.blueletterbible.org/Comm/torrey_ra/fundamentals/79.cfm

"G1392 - doxazō - Strong's Greek Lexicon (nkjv)." Blue Letter Bible. Accessed 30 May, 2023. https://www.blueletterbible.org/lexicon/g1392/nkjv/tr/0-1/

Henry, Matthew. "Commentary on John 18 by Matthew Henry." Blue Letter Bible. Last Modified 1 Mar, 1996. https://www.blueletterbible.org/Comm/mhc/Jhn/Jhn_018.cfm

"Expositor's Greek Testament." John 19:1. Bible Hub. Accessed May 30, 2023. https://biblehub.com/commentaries/john/19-1.htm

Guzik, David. "Study Guide for John 19 by David Guzik." Blue Letter Bible. Last Modified 6/2022. https://www.blueletterbible.org/comm/guzik_david/study-guide/john/john-19.cfm

"G991 - blepō - Strong's Greek Lexicon (kjv)." Blue Letter Bible. Accessed 30 May, 2023. https://www.blueletterbible.org/lexicon/g991/kjv/tr/0-1/

"G2334 - theōreō - Strong's Greek Lexicon (kjv)." Blue Letter Bible. Accessed 30 May, 2023. https://www.blueletterbible.org/lexicon/g2334/kjv/tr/0-1/

"G1492 - eidō - Strong's Greek Lexicon (kjv)." Blue Letter Bible. Accessed 30 May, 2023. https://www.blueletterbible.org/lexicon/g1492/kjv/tr/0-1/

Printed in the United States
by Baker & Taylor Publisher Services